428.42 Wagner, Rudolph F.
WAG
Helping the
wordblind

182539

HELPING THE WORDBLIND:
Effective Intervention Techniques for
Overcoming Reading Problems
in Older Students

HELPING THE WORDBLIND:
Effective Intervention
Techniques for Overcoming
Reading Problems
in Older Students

Rudolph F. Wagner, Ph. D.

The Center for Applied Research in Education, Inc.
West Nyack, New York 10994

Library of Congress Cataloging in Publication Data

Wagner, Rudolph F
  Helping the wordblind.

  Bibliography: p.
  Includes index.
  1. Reading--Remedial teaching. 2. Tutors and
tutoring. I. Title.
LB1050.5.W26   428'.4'2   75-35586
ISBN 0-87628-389-X

Printed in the United States of America

About the Author

Rudolph F. Wagner, Ph.D., has been actively involved in elementary and secondary education for more than 20 years as an educational psychologist and specialist in specific learning disabilities. Dr. Wagner came to the United States in 1949 and is currently Chief Psychologist of the Richmond (Virginia) Public Schools. He also is a member of the adjunct faculties at Virginia Commonwealth University and the University of Richmond, as well as an instructor for the American Academy of Professional Psychology, New York. He is an internationally recognized consultant in the field of dyslexia and related learning disorders.

Dr. Wagner holds an M.A. degree from the University of Richmond, and a Ph.D. degree in Counseling Psychology from the George Washington University. His earlier training was done at the Institut für Psychotherapie in Stuttgart, West Germany. He is also a Diplomate in School Psychology, American Academy of Professional Psychology.

Among Dr. Wagner's contributions to the professional literature are a book entitled *Dyslexia and Your Child* (New York: Harper & Row, 1971) and a teacher's manual entitled *Teaching Phonics with Success* (Johnstown, Pa.; Mafex Associates, 1969). He is a frequent contributor to professional journals and actively engages in research in learning disabilities and related problems.

About This Book

While the dilemma of poor readers in our secondary schools today is well documented and reflected in appalling statistics, most aids dealing with diagnosis and remediation of reading problems concentrate on elementary school children. Few works are available which deal primarily with the specific problems of poor readers in our middle and senior high schools and show teachers ways to help older students with their reading difficulties. *Helping the Wordblind* seeks to meet this obvious need for new techniques and materials to help remediate the reading problems of these older students who are found in our middle and senior high schools reading at the second and third grade level.

This book focuses specifically on the problems of poor readers in their adolescence or early adulthood, wherever they can be found today. Many are in classrooms but deriving far fewer benefits than they could from the curricular fare. Others have left school prematurely and are struggling in low-level positions because they have trouble with reading.

The book is concerned particularly with older readers who have the potential to read on average or near-average levels given proper remediation and a fresh foundation, but who are unable to function on such levels now. It is not concerned with the unmotivated student or the "slow learner" whose mental ability level is significantly below average or borderline and who would be expected to read below grade level.

Written primarily for secondary school reading teachers, reading specialists, or resource teachers, the book should also prove valuable to school administrators, supervisors, school counselors, special education teachers, teachers in reading clinics specializing in the remediation of learning disabilities (dyslexia), and all other educators concerned with older readers who still need elementary level reading development.

The aim of renewed reading instruction for older but low-level readers can hardly be complete mastery of the reading process. These poor readers have been unable to benefit from conventional reading instruction in the past and should not be confronted again with the same instructional approaches by which they failed miserably. The immediate goal, then, must be to pick up fragmentary segments of learning gleaned in the past and to work towards improvement and independence in reading so that these students can function as readers and partake in our culture and society where reading is an essential part of day-to-day living. A *functional* reader is able to read the headlines in the newspaper, can read the items on a simple questionnaire or simple passages in magazines and books. Effective reading instruction will assist the student in reading to his greatest potential provided his motivation is once again kindled and the relevance of his reading skills to real life is clearly shown.

Teachers will find the following to be especially helpful features of this book:

(1) *Immediacy of Help:* The book details practical ways to provide the student with help, *here and now.* Included are a variety of new remedial techniques which avoid the conventional approaches that have failed with this student in the past.

(2) *Availability of Resource Materials:* The methods and techniques suggested in the book are practical and inexpensive, requiring no complicated teaching machines or equipment.

(3) *Relevance of Content:* Particular care has been taken to select textual reading and exercises that are geared to the specific interests of adolescents and young adult readers.

(4) *Tutorial Relationship:* The basic remedial approach and strategy detailed in the book focuses on a tutor-

student relationship, preferably on a one-to-one basis. Only an intimate relationship and private setting will help the older student overcome the inhibitions and defenses built up in response to repeated failure.

(5) *Development of Self-Confidence:* The book stresses ways to help the poor reader build a stronger self-image and regain lost self-confidence. This may often be accomplished indirectly; i.e., by selecting appropriate tasks which he can master.

(6) *Organization of Remedial Groups and Self-Help:* Although the major thrust is on individualized remediation, the book includes some guidelines and suggestions for organizing small groups of poor readers for more efficient remedial instructions. The suggested approaches also emphasize self-help and reliance on available resources in school, home, and community, to bring assistance to people who otherwise may not have been reached.

Throughout the book, references to teachers and tutors will be made by employing the feminine pronoun referring to teachers of both sexes. This is done for the sake of brevity and clarity as a customary style of writing rather than as demonstrated prejudice toward our male readers.

A final word about the title of this book, *Helping the Wordblind,* is in order. It was in 1877 that a German physician, Adolf Kussmaul, introduced the actual terms "worddeafness" and "wordblindness" (*Worttaubheit und Wortblindheit*) in the literature. Kussmaul was one of the outstanding figures in German medicine in the nineteenth century and focused some of his professional attention on speech pathology and related brain functions. James Hinshelwood, an ophthalmologist in Glasgow, also made an important contribution to the study of reading disability. In 1896, he wrote about wordblindness and visual memory and remained a "torchlighter" in this field for over two decades. Other pioneers in the field were Rudolf Berlin in Germany who first coined the word "dyslexia" and Samuel Orton in this country, a neurologist, who used the word "strephosymbolia" to describe the peculiar reading habits he observed in his young clients.

It is in humble deference to these early pioneers in the field of reading disability that this book has been written. The term *wordblindness* seems to describe our young but poor readers: While they have eyes to see, they cannot read the printed word.

Rudolph F. Wagner

ACKNOWLEDGMENTS

No author ever creates a book without relying on previously published materials and expressed ideas. This book is no exception. Grateful acknowledgment is herewith expressed to all who helped to make *Helping the Wordblind* a reality. Tentative versions of the manuscript were tried in various situations and with the patient and understanding help of teachers, parents, and students.

In order not to dissociate an author or contributor from his original work, acknowledgments are made wherever the contribution occurs in the text. Many professional educators willingly gave their permission and consent to quote their contributions and cite references where indicated. It is believed that their ideas and comments greatly enhanced the final production of the manuscript for this book.

R.F.W.

Contents

1

Looking at
a Grave Problem

Nobody will deny that a man or woman who cannot read well is handicapped in our fast-paced and progressive culture. Perhaps we have placed too much emphasis on reading at the expense of other academic skills taught in school, such as spelling, writing, or arithmetic, but the problem is still a very real one: A young person who cannot read at all, or is a functional reader at best, who creeps and labors at a third grade level performance, must not expect to find open doors at the employment office. And the older our poor reader is, the more frustrating the whole situation becomes for him.

Evidence that poor readers exist in our society comes to us in many ways, if not directly through personal experiences as students, teachers, or parents. This chapter presents evidence in two ways: by statistical documentation and by case examples. It also outlines some of the warning signals of poor reading, especially as they apply to older students and adolescents whose dilemma has not yet been detected.

STATISTICAL EVIDENCE OF POOR READING

In a survey conducted in 1969 by the Health, Education and Welfare (HEW) Advisory Committee on Dyslexia and Related Reading Disorders, the introductory remarks in the preface of the study put the message into crisp and clear language: "Eight million children in America's elementary and secondary schools today will not learn to read adequately. One child in seven is handicapped in his ability to acquire essential reading skills. This phenomenon pervades all segments of our society—black and white, boys and girls, the poor and the affluent."[1] And if the message is not clear enough, here is another quotation from the same source: "The enrollment in the primary and secondary grades of our public schools is 51,500,000. The average cost per child per year is $696. If one child in 20 (5 percent) is not promoted, the national loss expressed in economic terms alone is $1.7 billion."

These figures help us appreciate the immense economic expense involved in the loss of a potential reader in our society. But we must also consider the tremendous cultural loss and deprivation of the poor reader himself, not to mention his poor self-image and personal as well as financial sacrifices.

Other sources of statistical information about disabled readers are equally impressive if not appalling. National surveys indicate that a minimum of 5 percent of all school age children (National Committee on Handicapped Children) to a maximum of 25 percent (U.S. Office of Education) of all children are unable to function normally because of some degree of reading difficulty.

The poor readers, whether children, adolescents, or adults, are forgotten people and are labeled by various terms: poor readers, dyslexics, pushouts and dropouts. They are considered academic failures, and potential failures in life. Many possess average and better intelligence, yet they cannot learn effectively through regular school programs. They are unable to fit the standard pattern set for them by society and educational

---

[1] *Reading Disorders in the United States.* Report of the HEW Secretary's National Advisory Committee on Dyslexia and Related Reading Disorders, August 1969.

institutions. They have suffered, and in most instances are still suffering, repeated frustrations and agony. Some of them already show early signs of maladjustment and are unable to function normally in society unless given special assistance of one kind or another. Some are on welfare rolls, others are engaged in pre-delinquent and delinquent behavior. Still others simply have fallen by the wayside of our human endeavor.

CASE EXAMPLES OF POOR READERS

Few follow-up studies are available which show the circumstances of poor readers after they leave school. Indications are that if reading problems are not straightened out before entering the world of work, it is clear that many will run into obstacles and embarrassing situations. For example, a young girl managed to land a job as a sales clerk in her home town upon leaving school. She did not work there for very long because somehow her sales slips were unreadable and contained many errors. Nor could she read instructions and messages given to her by her supervisors. It was as if she were "wordblind," as someone once described the condition. For instance, instead of reading or writing $14.84 on the sales ticket, she might enter $41.48 in a column; i.e., she reversed the figures. Needless to say, no business can withstand this kind of faulty reading and writing for very long.

Another case comes to mind, that of a bright boy who was an excellent machinist but who could never take advantage of any promotions in the shop where he worked because he could not fill out a questionnaire or report form. He was very good in carrying out instructions if they were given to him orally, but when the same instructions were handed to him on a piece of paper he was unable to read them accurately, causing misunderstandings between worker and employer. The same young man had once tried to apply for a commission in the army because of his excellent conduct and high intelligence, but he was denied the promotion as soon as it became known that he was reading on the third grade level. His vita was full of spelling errors and corrections. He was unable to read questions on various application forms. His disappointment was grave and consequential for his entire future. His dilemma was intensified after he married when his son began to read. His own inadequacy represented a tremendous threat to him as the father.

In still another instance a young high school student, also a poor reader, had managed to obtain a part-time job in a grocery store. All he had to do was put up stock at night. Not able to read labels properly, he would do all right if the label also showed a picture along with the words. A picture of green peas along with the words *Green Peas* were easily associated, but when the label did not show any pictorial clues, *marmalade* and *margarine* ended up on the wrong shelves. The part-time job did not last very long. Regretfully, the store manager had to let our young man go.

Two case histories are reported by William Mulligan, Chief Probation Officer at Sonoma County Probation Office in California. They are presented here, with Mr. Mulligan's kind permission.

(1) "Last year we screened a 15-year-old boy who was in the tenth grade and was having problems at home because of his extremely poor attitude. He was in a slow class and was failing all courses and had been expelled from one class that was being taught by a teacher who was a former military man and had indicated to the mother that he knew how to handle these types of problems. This particular boy had an IQ of 127 and was reading on the fifth month of a college freshman, but was dysgraphic.* We wrote up our screening test and referred him to a neurologist who has a child study and therapy center. This young man received specific tutoring from a remedial teacher at the center and passed his final exams with As and Bs. He is continuing his remedial training and is now in regular classes obtaining all As and Bs and has a completely different outlook on life and is very pleasant and no longer has any problems at home or in school."

(2) "Approximately seven years ago, we found a 15-year-old boy who was reading at the fourth month level of kinder-

---

*Evidenced as a disability in handwriting (Author's comment).

garten and had an IQ of 96 and was in the ninth grade. He was finally released from continuing school at the age of 18 and in the tenth grade. He made serious attempts to gain employment, even to the point of working for nothing just to gain experience. However, when it was discovered that he could neither read nor write, he was fired. He is now almost 22 years of age and has been declared totally and permanently disabled for life and is receiving $140 a month from the Social Service Department's Aid to the Totally Disabled Budget. Recently his girl friend called me to seek assistance in that he is drinking up his money to blank out his failure in life. If that $140 per month had been expended in his early years for prescriptive teaching, he could now be a successful citizen, because even with his handicap he had not committed any offense other than being truant, for which we never punished him. Unfortunately, we didn't have funds or program to help him either."

Chief Probation Officer William Mulligan's two case illustrations need no comment.

A COMPLETE CASE HISTORY

1. Background Information

J.M., a 21-year-old man, was born somewhat prematurely but with no signs of any abnormalities. He struggled through the elementary grades of a public school, always behind in his academic work but always finding a kind soul who would promote him to the next grade. In high school he was given special consideration and he had to work twice as hard to keep up with his classmates. During the latter part of his high school years, his parents separated and were later divorced. There is one brother in the family, older than J.M., and one older sister, both having done well in regular public school and later on, in college. In spite of many academic setbacks and failures, J.M. obtained a high school diploma. As his brother and sister had done, he decided to go to college. During the first year in college he failed subjects closely related to reading and writing, such as Freshman English and History. He was told by the Dean that he could not return the following semester, but he was reinstated two years later after returning from overseas duty.

Again his grades were low (D's and F's) and he was placed on probation. Poorly advised by the faculty due to the undetected nature of his learning problem, J.M. enrolled in courses which were over his head, like neurophysiology. No vocational guidance was given during this time. He finally dropped out of college because of failing grades.

Soon after leaving college, J.M. entered the world of work as a clerk. Through some fortuitous circumstances, his brother met a teacher at Sunday School one day and discussed J.M.'s dilemma with her. The teacher recommended a psychoeducational evaluation for specific learning disabilities since she herself was a teacher of dyslexic children and knew their symptoms well. The evaluation resulted in a diagnosis of Specific Learning Disability focusing on reading, spelling, and handwriting.

2. Initial Evaluation Data

Assessment of J.M.'s intelligence revealed a young man who functioned on average levels of mental ability. However, there was a decided difference between what he could express verbally and what he could show without using words. His Verbal I.Q. was actually above average, while his Performance I.Q. was below average. There also was some suspicion of a mild cerebral dysfunction, without obvious organic impairments. His dominance for sidedness was left for hands, confused for eyes, and left for feet. This is also referred to as a "mixed or crossed dominance pattern" which may have a negative effect on academic performance even though the condition is of no diagnostic significance in itself. He did not reverse any letters or words, but got confused when words with consonant clusters were presented visually (e.g., scram, script, Episcopal, statistics, etc.). He was able to discriminate sounds by ear (good auditory discrimination) and had no visual acuity defects of any kind. Personality adjustment was within normal limits but his self-concept was very low due to repeated academic failures.

J.M.'s handwriting was judged poor in quality and might be related to his mild cerebral dysfunction. Spelling showed errors, especially in letter transposition within a word (trail for trial, for example). Oral reading was fluent when words were presented in context, but when words were presented individually, oral reading was quite below expectation. He obtained a Reading Grade Equivalent of 6.8 (late sixth grade), with Spelling at 7.0 (beginning of seventh grade).

3. Diagnostic Impression

In the absence of any gross pathological findings in the realm of cognitive and emotional functioning, other than subtest variability on the intelligence test and secondary emotional reactions to a primary learning handicap, the diagnostic impression was one of Specific Learning Disability (dyslexia), affecting reading, spelling, and handwriting and, to some extent, comprehension. Arithmetic reasoning was at normal levels.

4. Remedial Prescription

J.M. was subsequently seen in individual sessions, on a once-a-week basis, for a period of approximately a year and a half. The sessions consisted of tutorial hours broken down into segments specifically designed for his deficiencies (see Chapter 7 for 15-minute modules). Methodological approaches varied, focusing on his reading, spelling, and writing deficiencies (see Chapters 4, 5, and 6 for remedial suggestions). In addition to remedial work in the academic realm, tutorial counseling for emotional support was employed to build up the low self-image (see Chapter 3). The basic approach was one of academic therapy; that is, a combination of academic remediation exercises and counseling.

5. Results

J.M.'s overall improvement ranged from satisfactory to remarkable progress, especially when the fact is considered that tutorial sessions were held only once a week during a period of 18 months, with time out for holidays and vacations. During this period, J.M. held a full-time job (programmer trainee) and attended two evening college courses which he passed at the end of each semester. His progress can be gleaned from Tables 1-1 and 1-2. Table 1-1 shows an increase of I.Q. scores, with a Full

Scale I.Q. jump of 13 points, which must be considered beyond practice effect implications. In reading, he gained better than three grade levels, while spelling improved only one and a half grade levels (see Table 1-2).

Table 1-1

Pre- and Post-Test Results on the Wechsler Adult Intelligence Scale (Two-Year Interval)

Period	Verbal IQ	Perf. IQ	Full IQ
Pre-	111	86	101
Post-	122	100	114
Difference (Gain)	+11	+14	+13

Table 1-2

Pre- and Post-Test Results on the Wide Range Achievement Test (Two-Year Interval)

Period	Reading Grade	Spelling Grade
Pre-	6.8	7.0
Post-	10.0	8.5
Difference (Gain)	+3.2	+1.5

The overall improvement is also reflected in J.M.'s drawing of a human figure, possibly indicative of an improved self-image (see Figures 1-1 and 1-2).

Marked improvement in fine motor coordination and visual perception is also evidenced in his performance on the Bender Visual Motor Gestalt Test (see Figure 1-3), where he now shows better ability in the copying of simple designs with accuracy

Figure 1-1

Initial Drawing of Human Figure

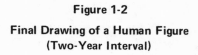

Figure 1-2

Final Drawing of a Human Figure
(Two-Year Interval)

Figure 1-3
Some Changes on the Bender Visual Motor Gestalt Test
(Two-Year Interval)

Card 1

Card 4

Card 8

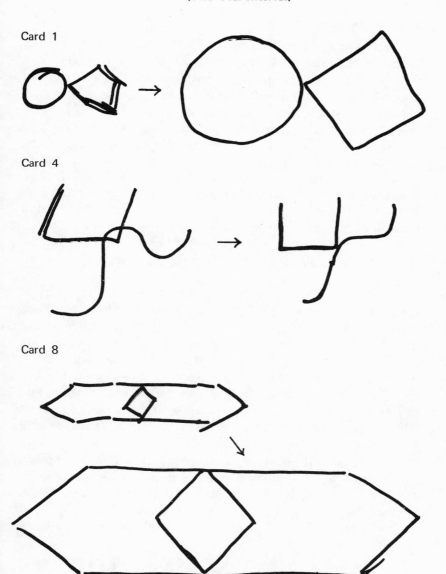

and better line drawing and orientation in space. No doubt, J.M.'s self-confidence was bolstered by the tutorial relationship and is also reflected in his test performances.

6. Conclusions

Considering the fact that J.M.'s reading and learning disability was detected late and had gone untreated for a prolonged period of time, his progress during the tutorial sessions was substantial. It allowed him to finish college and obtain a Master's degree. Instead of making failing and near-failing grades, he ended up with passing grades (B average). At the same time, he was able to hold a full-time job which involved an emphasis on mathematical and mechanical skills while de-emphasizing linguistic factors. Vocational guidance was evidently a very important component of tutorial counseling. J.M.'s life became bearable without the fear of academic and social failure and embarrassment.

CHARACTERISTICS OF POOR READERS

Usually, poor readers have good hearing and good vision, even though these sensory modalities might have been corrected in the past or should now be corrected by hearing aids or eye glasses if found deficient. Good hearing and good vision are called auditory and visual acuity, respectively, and are basic to the ability to hear and see well. Professionals can readily test these two sensory modalities with appropriate examinations and instruments. The results of these tests would rule out any defect which might exist in these areas or interfere with normal functioning. But there is more to reading than having the ability to see and hear. In many cases, poor reading is due not so much to a sensory deficit, as to a deficiency in the way information is taken in from the outside; i.e., visual and auditory perception. We may see but not see accurately and be able to interpret what we see. We may hear, but not be able to discriminate between two different sounds.

But what if we do not find the causes of poor reading? What if professional help is not available, or not forthcoming?

By analogy, we would not leave an injured person unattended or unaided even though every effort is being made to seek help from competent professionals. There are diseases of the body, such as diabetes, where there is relatively little known about the causes of the disease but where help can be administered and lives saved. Helping does not necessarily imply curing, but it may enable the person to survive and to control the condition, at least. Thus we can help the poor reader to improve his condition and his lot even though the etiology, or cause, of his poor reading performance is not known to us for the time being. The fact remains that he *is* a poor reader. Frequently, poor reading remains undetected during a person's entire school career, and even beyond, in college and at work. The poor reader keeps on failing and suffering, and develops emotional reactions to his primary learning problem which often show up disguised as a behavior problem or emotional hangup.

Poor readers exist "from the cradle to the grave." The author has encountered too many unhappy, puzzled people who did not know why they were failing, why they couldn't read like others. And among these fine people, there were insurance salesmen who could not pass their professional examinations, college students who flunked one course after the other, high school students who had to repeat their last year in school, sales clerks who rang up $41 on the sales register instead of $14, and bright young students who were denied rewarding careers as physicians or lawyers because they couldn't read well enough to measure up to the tests they were supposed to pass. All because of poor reading.

The nature of dyslexia in adulthood, a term for specific reading disabilities, was described by the late Harold Dannenhower in an article titled "Teaching Adults with Specific Language Disability," (*Bulletin of the Orton Society*, XXII, 1972). Dannenhower stated that if reading problems have not been detected in childhood the adult dyslexic still has the same problem we meet in children, but with an intensification of the social and emotional consequences resulting from added years of failure, frustration, and hopelessness. These adolescents and adults have developed defense mechanisms against demands to read and spell. They have surrounded themselves with an assortment of barricades. They are perfectly capable of completely turning off or ignoring anything, anywhere, that is printed. Happily, Dannenhower concluded, as success becomes possible, the old defenses usually give way.

DIFFERENCES AMONG POOR READERS

Poor reading is a universal term accepted by educators and the public alike, yet when we look at the different kinds of people around us we realize that they are individually quite different from each other. Even twins are not exactly alike. In the same way, poor reading is not always exactly alike. Two boys of the same age may have attended the same school and have had the same teacher all along, but their reading achievement can differ markedly. What introduces these differences is a variety of factors, both intrinsic and extrinsic, such as genetic endowment, levels of motivation, cultural experiences, or parental expectancies. Even when the same teaching methods are used, two different students may perceive them quite differently.

Again, the kind of poor reader we talk about here is not merely the underachieving or lazy adolescent who went through school without trying. But if he now reads significantly below grade level, he too may have to be considered a poor reader. For example, if a 15-year-old boy with average or above intelligence and all things considered normal reads at the ninth grade level while he is placed in the ninth grade, we would say that he is a "normal" reader. But if a boy or girl with these same qualifications reads at the sixth grade level, we can speak of a poor reader, regardless of the causes. The difference between expected and actual reading level has to be significant. This question of expectancy versus actual reading performance will be taken up again in the next chapter where more precise definitions will be offered. We differentiate also between underachievers, those who just don't read up to par, and those who have difficulty in acquiring the techniques of reading from the start. We are not dealing here with just "lazy" people or those who have fallen behind because they did not apply themselves, but with a *specific* learning disability focusing on reading. What are some of the tell-tale signs we have to look for in these poor readers? The checklist below may be used for a first rough diagnostic screening, to be followed with more precise tests to pinpoint the problems more specifically.

A teacher or tutor may use this checklist to screen an individual student or an entire group. The teacher might read the statements to the person and then check off significant findings, or he or she may read them to the entire class and provide a simple checklist with boxes where the answers can be written in by the individual students in the classroom. This first screening procedure is not necessarily fool-proof because some individuals may, by the very nature of their problem, be highly defensive and not give true answers to the questions or statements. Others might get confused, especially when asked to mark answer sheets. Checklists also are not 100 percent fool-proof inasmuch as they merely represent a sieve, as it were, through which some people might slip and go unrecognized, while others are "false positives"; i.e., they were caught in the net but are really not good catches. Someone in the group might think he is a poor speller just because he once got an "F" on a quiz when he did not study the night before the test.

WARNING SIGNS OF POOR READING

Note that not all of the signs enumerated below have to be present in one individual to strengthen the suspicion that he is an individual with a specific reading disability or general reading problem. It takes *several* signs to make an individual eligible for further investigation of his reading problem.

1. *Reversal Errors.* During the early school years, especially the early elementary grades, letter and word reversals occur frequently, such as "b" for "d," "was" for "saw," or "aminal" for "animal." Difficulties exist especially with consonant blends contained in words such as "plot" for "pilot," "title" for "tilt," or "clot"

for "colt." Some of these reversals can be found in adolescents, and even adults if the errors were untreated and no specific remediation was attempted.

2. *Above Age for Grade Placement.* Barring below average intelligence, a student may have repeated one or several grades in order to catch up with his poor reading. Some of these students become dropouts or "push-outs," during their middle or high school years. Their present reading level is significantly below expectancy for age and intelligence, usually one or two grades below expectancy. However, in the early elementary grades, such as kindergarten and first grade, this difference is less pronounced but may still be a warning signal. Failing to read at normal level continues and becomes worse in later grades.

3. *Secondary Emotional Reactions.* Emotional reactions, secondary in nature, become apparent as failure to read becomes pronounced and prolonged. These secondary emotional reactions may take the form of withdrawal, aggression, defensiveness, clowning, inattentiveness, daydreaming, and so forth. All these reactions can be emotionally based maneuvers to cover up for poor reading.

4. *Negative Visual and Auditory Examinations.* Just because one had his eyes or ears checked by a competent professional does not necessarily mean that no specific reading disability exists. Many poor readers have gone the route from one professional examination to the other, but their reading disability still remained undetected.

5. *Confusion in Spatial Orientation.* In addition to left-right discrimination problems, there may be other signs of poor orientation in space. For example, a student might not be able to say the days of the week in proper sequence, may confuse a series of digits, or get mixed up with yesterday and tomorrow, or frequently displace his or her keys, handbag, or other objects of daily use.

6. *Significant Incidents During Early Childhood.* Before, during, or immediately after birth many things can go wrong. Prolonged labor, difficulties in delivery, or infantile infections and diseases are "red flags" which may relate to poor reading. Injuries sustained during falls or high fever accompanying childhood diseases are other warning signals which should be carefully noted.

7. *Hereditary Endowment.* The reading problem may "run in the family;" i.e., there may be a history of hereditary or genetically caused problems. Although hereditary factors are not always assumed to be a major cause of reading disability, some poor reading varieties are suspected of being sex-linked and may be passed down from parent to offspring. The condition seems to affect males more than females, in an approximate ratio of 4 to 1, respectively.

8. *Physical Behavior Problems.* Hyperactivity, fidgetiness, inattentiveness, and distractibility all are considered high-risk signals of reading problems. There also is clumsiness in holding a pencil, or dropping a glass of orange juice at the breakfast table more often than just by accident. Under this category also might fall clumsiness on the yard, playground, or in sports, like walking along a wooden beam, catching a ball, or coordinating hands and eyes properly during manual activities. These symptoms are often mistaken for behavior problems of the more notorious variety that involve doing malicious things.

9. *Speech Delays or Difficulties.* While difficulties with speech are not necessarily indicative of a reading problem, the incidence of such problems is higher in poor readers. Baby talk at a time when children of the same age have long outgrown such immature patterns, or difficulty with certain words like spaghetti (pasghetti), statistics (stastistics), pajamas (japamas), and others, all tell-tales to the observer.

10. *Avoidance Games.* Poor readers who are in their adolescent years often have tried desperately to adjust

to their poor reading conditions and have invented
"games" to avoid unpleasant situations. People who
excuse themselves at the sight of a book, begin to tell a
joke when reading should be done instead, or indulge
in peculiar rituals when confronted with reading tasks
must be suspected as potential poor readers.

Chapter Summary

*There is abundant statistical evidence that poor
reading is a widespread learning disability among
elementary and secondary students as well as adults.
Case histories from professional workers and probation officers support this evidence. Poor readers
have many problems accompanying their failure to
acquire sound reading skills. They also show signs of
secondary emotional reactions.*

*The vigilant and trained teacher can readily
identify such poor readers in the classroom. Familiarity with the various "warning signals" of poor
reading may help him or her in locating children and
adolescents with specific learning problems. Early
detection of reading difficulties is important. The
dilemma of poor readers intensifies as they grow
older and face continued failure in school, at work,
and in life. Their situation calls for refined diagnostic
and remedial tools to help salvage potentially normal
youngsters.*

Scott isn't stupid. But it took a smart teacher to recognize it.

Public awareness of learning disabilities is reflected in this advertisement. Reproduced with kind permission of Metropolitan Life, New York, N.Y.

2

Assessing the Reading Problem

Chapter 1 presented a list of warning signals of severe reading problems. While these signals are very useful in the detection of problems, they do not identify all problem readers. Many students drop out of school prematurely and we have no chance to observe them. The warning signals also do not tell us much about just what caused the reading difficulties. There may be instances where the cause or causes remain obscure or unknown, or the technical aspects involved in causative factors may be in the domain of the professional only. Regardless of the causes, teachers as well as parents will concern themselves primarily with the behavioral—that is, observable—aspects of poor reading. It is at that level that intervention must start and can be most effective.

CAUSES OF POOR READING

A brief look at some of the more prevalent theories will provide the reader with an overview of causative factors in poor reading. In some poor readers, the maturational development lags behind that of the average student. They simply are not ready for reading instruction; they show signs of immaturity in several facets of human growth and development. Neurological dysfunctions are often cited as causing poor reading. Such conditions, at least, contribute to the deficiencies. Perceptual deficits frequently are pinpointed as playing a role in poor reading. These perceptual deficits can be found in the visual area but other sensory modalities, such as auditory, tactile, and kinesthetic, also contribute to the malfunctioning reading process. The subject of causative factors in poor reading is still very controversial and far from being resolved. Only recently have we turned to the problems of older students whose learning problems have remained undetected and for whom remedial techniques have not been fully developed. Before these adolescents can be helped, however, some form of assessment is needed to pinpoint their specific problems.

ASSESSMENT PROCEDURES AND TECHNIQUES

After a student has come to our attention because of a suspected reading problem, the next step is to assess the problem areas in order to make remediation more precise and effective. In adolescents and adults, the condition may have been allowed to linger. For this reason especially, remedial intervention has to be immediate and appropriate to the condition. Often, professional help is either not readily available or it clusters in urban areas, while rural or isolated regions lack appropriate facilities to help these students.

The screening devices presented here must be accepted as a rough assessment which serves as a preliminary survey rather than a precise evaluation; however, if certain areas of poor reading on the behavioral level are looked into, they will guide the teacher in remedial intervention. The areas where some form of assessment is needed to pinpoint deficiencies are the following:

1. Level of intelligence
2. Reading level

3. Physical and related factors

4. Background information

The assessment approach outlined here does not exclude more thorough and professional examinations. It simply serves the purpose of initial screening, and, what is all important, provides a starting point which, hopefully, will become a turning point in the life of a person who has suffered from poor reading. There is much to gain and little to lose!

1. Assessing Level of Intelligence

The level of intelligence is closely related to the ability to read in terms of predicting a person's reading achievement. A retarded child can hardly be expected to read at the same level as a normal child of the same chronological age, and a person with superior intelligence is usually expected to read on above-average reading levels when compared with a person of normal or average intelligence. The Academic Expectancy Chart (Figure 2-1) reproduced on page 40 will give you a rough indication of what to expect from a given person with regard to his reading level when age and intelligence levels are known.

Under ordinary circumstances, the expected grade level would also be the grade placement of a student. However, many students have dropped out of school or left it prematurely so that the grade placement is of no consequence. If a person reads below the expected level when taking his age and intelligence level into consideration, we must regard him as a poor reader who apparently does have more intellectual potential but for some reason or other has not been able to reach it due to interfering variables such as lack of instruction, perceptual deficits, or other as yet unknown factors. Usually, one to two years below the expected level is considered significant to establish the verdict of a reading problem or deficiency.

The gap between expected and actual reading level widens as the person grows older and his condition remains unremediated. A child in the first grade reading on the 1.5 grade level at the end of the school year is only half a grade below the achievement of his average peers, but half a year must be considered significant since the deficiency is relative to his age.

Figure 2-1

ACADEMIC EXPECTANCY CHART

Classif. ⟶	MENTALLY RETARDED (TRAINABLE)	MENTALLY RETARDED (EDUCABLE)	MENTALLY RETARDED (EDUCABLE)	BORDERLINE SLOW LEARNER	SLOW LEARNER	NORMAL
Dependency ⟶	Dependent	Semi-Dependent		Independent		
Skill Level ⟶	Unskilled	Unskilled	Semi-Skilled		Skilled	
IQ Range ⟶	Below 50	51-65	66-75	76-80	81-89	90-110
CA ↓	Expected Academic Level			(Grade Equivalent)		
6-0— 6-9	R	R	R	R	R/1	1
7-0— 7-9	R	R	R	R/1	1	2
8-0— 8-9	R	R	1	1	2	3
9-0— 9-9	R	R	1	1/2	2/3	4
10-0—10-9	R	1	2	2	3	5
11-0—11-9	1	2	2	3	4	6
12-0—12-9	1	2	3	3/4	4/5	7
13-0—13-9	1	3	3	4	5	8
14-0—14-9	2	3	4	5	6	9
15-0—15-9	2	4	4/5	5/6	6/7	10
16-0—16-9	2	4	5	6	7/8	11

LEGEND: CA = Chronological Age
6-9 = 6 years and 9 months
R = Readiness Program
2 = Grade Assignment in School

This simplified Academic Expectancy Chart is based on a more detailed chart published by the Bureau for Children with Retarded Mental Development, New York, N.Y. Originally covering a range of IQ's 50-80, it has been extrapolated upward to encompass the IQ's up to 110.

On the other hand, an adolescent in the twelfth grade may be reading on the tenth grade level and might be able to manage his

assignments fairly well even though his efficiency would improve if his reading were closer to his actual grade placement
level.

Most people do not realize that intelligence and IQ are two
different things and should not be used interchangeably as
terms. Intelligence is a concept, something that cannot be
touched. On the other hand, an Intelligence Quotient (IQ) is a
ratio based on chronological, or actual, age (CA) and a series of
tests or tasks on which the individual is compared with others
(Norm) yielding a measure of Mental Age (MA). MA is then
divided by CA and the product multiplied by 100 to remove the
digit and get a whole number. Thus, an IQ as a score is once
or twice removed from the actual data and only allows us to
infer what the person's real intelligence level may be.

It is not always possible to obtain a valid measure of a
person's intelligence level. Individually administered intelligence
tests are usually considered more valid than group test results. If
no indications of an IQ score are available, perhaps a former
teacher or guidance counselor of the school last attended by the
student could give some indication of the category in which the
person belongs. Essentially what is needed in the assessment
process is an estimate as to whether a person is below average,
average, or above average, rather than a definite score. In order
to read at expected grade levels, minimally average intelligence
is required. Otherwise, one must lower one's expectancy of the
person's reading performance. Here are two examples to illustrate the point:

Example A: A young man at the age of 17 and with an IQ of
99 (average) should ordinarily be in the twelfth grade in high
school. His reading level can be calculated by subtracting 5
from 17, the 5 standing for the five years before he
entered kindergarten. Under normal circumstances—that is,
not having repeated a grade or coming from a severely
deprived home situation—he should be reading on the twelfth
grade level. Any number of grades below this expected level
would be regarded as a reading deficit. For example, if the

young man reads at the eighth grade level, he would be behind in reading achievement by four grades, a significant reading problem.

Example B: A girl in the eighth grade reads on the sixth grade level, as measured by a reliable test. Ordinarily this would mean a reading problem because she is reading two grades below expectancy. But let us assume that the girl has subnormal intelligence. In this case, her present sixth-grade reading level could be expected because of her low mental ability (see Figure 2-1). One would also have to make allowances for possible retention in one grade or more, making the deficit even greater than shown. On the other hand, if the girl's intelligence were above average (she had an IQ score of 118 on a given test), then we could expect even more from her. Her present reading level could be regarded as a greater deficit than under normal conditions.

The term "under normal conditions" implies that circumstances may not always be normal in any given situation. There are some children who read at the expected level (or even above) in spite of subnormal intelligence. This might be explained on the basis of having a superior phonetic word attack skill or an enriched home atmosphere where remedial help was offered by the parents. In another situation, a person may have acquired the basic word analysis skills (i.e., the mechanics of reading), but lags behind in comprehension of what was read. Such a condition will be further discussed in Chapter 6. At any rate, consideration of intelligence in the reading process will serve as a guide—as a relative rather than an absolute ingredient.

To help you make judgments about intellectual functioning related to reading skills, the following IQ ranges will serve as a guide for categorization of intelligence levels:

IQ Range	*Category*
Below 75	Mentally Retarded
76 to 89	Slow Learner (Below Average)
90 to 109	Average
110–119	Above Average
120 and above	Superior

The Academic Expectancy Chart on page 40 provides a somewhat finer breakdown of intelligence categories.

2. Assessing Reading Level

After estimating a student's intelligence level, the next step is to find out how well he can read. One way of finding out is to sit down with him and let him read out loud. We can readily notice the mistakes he makes, his hesitations when he tries to attack difficult words, or certain reversal errors. Many teachers ask the student to read various samples written at different grade levels. This provides only a crude estimate and requires too much time for what we get out of it.

Another way is to present the student with a graded list of single words and look for the point at which he begins to make mistakes consistently. This is the so-called word recognition test and it is widely used. It actually taps a kind of artificial reading since normal reading material contains sentences and not single words. The word recognition is given orally only. When reading passages, the reader depends not only on his word attack skills, either by phonic or visual structural analysis, but also receives valuable contextual clues; i.e., he makes guesses and draws inferences from meaning.

It would be a more natural test if the student were given whole sentences to read from graded material. Such a simple test is presented on pages 45 to 51. The graded passages (Figure 2-2) are printed on separate pages, two grades to one page, Grades K through 12, so that they can readily be used as the actual test materials. A separate form is also reproduced on pages 53 and 55 to provide a record of results and a protocol to follow (See Figure 2-3). An assessment of reading errors can be found under the heading of Background Information, below.

Instructions for Administering and Scoring the Estimate of Reading Grade Level

Instructions

The purpose of the Estimate of Reading Grade Level is to give the teacher or tutor an estimate of the student's reading grade level before remedial teaching is begun. Reading passages are presented by grade level in ascending order, Grades K through 12. Remedial instructions must start where the student begins to show difficulty with his reading. The passages are given within the context of short sentences and will provide the teacher with valuable clues to phonetic sensitivity in work attack skills and reversal tendencies in addition to an estimate of grade level. The Reading Estimate should be used as a guide for the teacher and not as a final judgment of the student's reading ability.

Figure 2-2

Sample Passages—
Estimate of Reading Grade Level

Level K

A   O   F   H   L   M   X

R   P   B   W   D   b   e

GOOD   LOOK

Level 1

Look, Sam, see the cat? It is my cat.
Sam can see it. Come here and see!
Can you see it? Go and see my cat!

Figure 2-2 (cont'd.)

Level 2

One boy said to his mother: I want to
go and play with my friend. Father
said: Go out and look at the dog!

Level 3

Father lives in the country. Many
people have nice boats and they can
sail on the lake. Please let sister come
along!

Figure 2-2 (cont'd.)

Level 4

Today is Monday. It has been snowing
outside. We can see the snowflakes
from our window. Come along for a
beautiful sleigh ride.

Level 5

Robert's brown dog performs difficult
tricks. The animal jumps over the
basket because his master has trained
him to obey quickly.

Figure 2-2 (cont'd.)

Level 6

Perhaps it is dangerous to tease wild beasts. They can become harmful if someone approaches them from behind. Trainers should be cautious and mindful.

Level 7

Many peoples live in Europe. Some are called Norwegians, Swedes, and Spaniards. Their customs are frequently quite peculiar to certain regions.

Figure 2-2 (cont'd.)

Level 8

> The early Greeks demonstrated that their remarkable culture was extremely high in development. Tedious research has produced revealing evidence.

Level 9

> Factories can potentially represent marvelous places for visitations of all kinds. Modern technological advances in manufacturing are demonstrated by industry in superior plants.

Figure 2-2 (cont'd.)

Level 10

The responsibility of diplomats should
entail extreme standards of excellence
and ethics. Diplomatic conduct should
rank superior to normally acceptable
levels.

Level 11

Celestial phenomena present a marvel
to pedestrians and the inquisitive
scientist alike. Techniques of
observation exist in abundance with
innovative instruments.

Figure 2-2 (cont'd.)

Level 12

Contemplations by early philosophers
repudiated the theories of their
predecessors but frequently advanced
parsimonious principles which were
considered phenomenal.

_____

Administering the Estimate

1. Establish a friendly relationship with the student to whom you are going to administer this estimate. Make him feel relaxed and reduce "test anxiety" to a minimum.

2. Ask the student to read the passages carefully as presented to him. Expose one passage at a time and cover up the rest of the sheet.

3. Pasting the passages in a small loose-leaf notebook, one passage on a page, will facilitate administration. Have a copy of the answer sheet for each student to be tested. (See Figure 2-3.)

4. Begin at a level where you feel the student is most comfortable and can read without making an error. If your judgment was too high, slip down a passage or two and move upward again until he reaches the break-off point as defined below.

5. Note the mistakes he makes in oral word recognition and mark them on the separate answer sheet by simply striking through the word or words he mispronounced or could not read at all. If time permits, the word's pronunciation should be written above the word which was misread. An example follows:

> Today is Monday. It ~~has~~ *had* been snowing ~~outside~~ *outdoors*. We ~~can~~ *could* see ~~the~~ *a* snowflakes ~~from~~ *for* our window. Come along for a beau*t*iful sleigh ride.

6. At the end of each passage, ask the student the Comprehension Question listed in the right column of the Answer Sheet (Figure 2-3). Make an X in the second (right) circle if he answers correctly. Even if the student does not answer correctly, the reading part should be continued for accuracy.

7. Discontinue the Estimate if the student makes at least *two word recognition errors* in a given passage for *two consecutive passages.* If only one mistake is made in a passage, continue the Estimate until the criterion of two mistakes in two consecutive passages is reached. In each paragraph, enter the number of mistakes (reading errors) in the first (left) circle.

Figure 2-3

Answer Sheet—

Estimate of Reading Grade Level

Student's Name _____ Date of Administration _____

Remarks: ┌─────── Record number of errors here

③ ⊘

                                    ▲─── Check for comprehension here

Grade Level	Text	Comprehension Question No. of Mistakes/Remarks
K	A O F H L M X R P B W D b e GOOD LOOK	Can you tell me two letters that you have just read? ○○
1	Look, Sam, see the cat? It is my cat. Sam can see it. Come here and see! Can you see it? Go and see my cat!	What kind of animal do we have in this story? ○○
2	One boy said to his mother: I want to go and play with my friend. Father said: Go out and look at the dog!	With whom did the boy in the story want to play? ○○
3	Father lives in the country. Many people have nice boats and they can sail on the lake. Please let sister come along!	Where can boats sail? ○○

Figure 2-3 (cont'd.)

4	Today is Monday. It has been snowing outside. We can see the snowflakes from our window. Come along for a beautiful sleigh ride.	Can you tell from the story how the weather is outside? ◯◯
5	Robert's brown dog performs difficult tricks. The animal jumps over the basket because his master has trained him to obey quickly.	What did Spot jump over after Robert trained him quickly? ◯◯
6	Perhaps it is dangerous to tease wild beasts. They can become harmful if someone approaches them from behind. Trainers should be cautious and mindful.	When can animals become dangerous? ◯◯
7	Many people live in Europe. Some are called Norwegians, Swedes, and Spaniards. Their customs are frequently quite peculiar to certain regions.	Can you name two different kinds of peoples in Europe? ◯◯
8	The early Greeks demonstrated that their remarkable culture was extremely high in development. Tedious research has produced revealing evidence.	What nation was at a high level of development in this story? ◯◯
9	Factories can potentially represent marvelous places for visitation of all kinds. Modern technological advances in manufacturing are demonstrated by industry in superior plants.	What can be demonstrated in modern manufacturing plants? ◯◯
10	The responsibility of diplomats should entail extreme standards of excellence and ethics. Diplomatic conduct should rank superior to normally acceptable levels.	What are the people called whose standards of ethics should be high? ◯◯

Figure 2-3 (cont'd.)

11	Celestial phenomena present a marvel to pedestrians and the inquisitive scientist alike. Techniques of observation exist in abundance with innovative instruments.	To what two groups of people are celestial phenomena a marvel? ◯◯
12	Contemplations by early philosophers repudiated theories of their predecessors but frequently advanced parsimonious principles which were considered phenomenal.	What kind of principles did early philosophers often advance after repudiating older theories? ◯◯

Scoring the Estimate

After the Estimate has been discontinued because the criterion or break-off point has been reached, immediate results are available to you. Computation of scores will produce an estimate of the student's Grade Level.

Here are three examples that illustrate the easy scoring system:

Example A   Up to

Level 8 = No mistakes   = 8.0
Level 9 = One mistake   = 0.5
Level 10 = Two mistakes   = 0.0
Level 11 = Three mistakes = 0.0

Total Reading Estimate   8.5 Grade Level

Example B   Up to

Level 3 = No mistakes   = 3.0
Level 4 = No mistakes   = 1.0
Level 5 = Two mistakes   = 0.0
Level 6 = One mistake   = 0.5
Level 7 = Three mistakes = 0.0
Level 8 = Eight mistakes = 0.0

Total Reading Estimate   4.5 Grade Level

Example C   Level K = Read all letters = 0.5
                 Level   1 = Six mistakes   = 0.0
                 Total Reading Estimate   0.5 Grade Level

1. Give a score of 1 for each paragraph read without mistakes. For example, if a student reads all paragraphs up to and including the one marked 5 in the left-hand column of the Estimate, and makes at least two mistakes in the paragraphs marked 6 and 7, he receives a total score of 5. The K Level receives no points in this computation. If a student can read all *letters* on the K Level but does not read the *words* (GOOD and LOOK), he receives a score of 0.5.

2. Give only half a point (0.5) for any passage where the student makes *one* mistake, adding it to the total count. For example, if a student read all words correctly at Grade 5 but made one mistake at the Grade 6 Level and two mistakes at Grades 7 and 8, his total score is 5 plus 0.5 = Total Score 5.5, or mid-fifth grade level.

3. Do not give credit for any passage which contains *two or more* errors. For example, if a student passes Grade 5 but makes two errors on Grade 6 level and also Grade 7 level, the Total Score is 5.0. If he passes Grade 5, makes two errors on Grade 6 but either passes Grade 7 or makes only one error, but then fails Grades 8 and 9 (two or more errors, the break-off criterion), his Grade Level would be 5.5 or 6.0, respectively, depending on whether he makes one or two errors on Grade 7 level. THE ONLY EXCEPTION IN SCORING IS AT THE K LEVEL: Give 0.5 for all letters read correctly, and 0.5 for the two *words* read correctly.

The Estimate is not recommended for use with kindergarten children because it is relatively insensitive at this level. However, the teacher can gain valuable clues from observing students' reading behavior at this level.

Additional clues for reading efficiency can be gleaned from the Estimate by briefly checking the student's comprehension. After each passage in the Estimate, the teacher asks the question printed in the right column of the Estimate and makes a check-mark if the student can answer the question correctly. Several failures in comprehension would indicate some difficulty in this area of reading skills worthy of investigation. Chapter 6 deals extensively with this important aspect of reading and lists remedial techniques for deficiencies in comprehension.

Interpretation and Remedial Implications

The final score will tell the teacher or tutor where instruction and remedial work have to start. The results will *not* tell the teacher what kind of techniques or methods to use since the Estimate primarily provides a quantitative measure. The quality of the reading must be ascertained by clinical observations or additional test instruments. Having an estimate of a student's grade level will avoid much trial-and-error work until a starting point for remedial work is finally reached. A brief case example may further illustrate the usefulness of the Estimate by commenting on instructional and remedial implications.

JAMES, 18 years of age and a dropout, was started out on the Estimate at the Grade 6 level by the teacher because it was known to her that he had dropped out of school in the sixth grade after several social promotions. He made two mistakes here, reading "careful" for cautious and "tamers" for trainers. Because of these mistakes he was next given Level 5 where he performed without fault. However, the teacher noted that he said "aminal" for animal. On Level 7 he had a difficult time. "Peculiar" was read particular, "customs" as customers, and "quite" as quiet. Level 8 proved an impossible hurdle for James. The Estimate was discontinued at this point because of two missed passages.

How do we evaluate James' reading performance? Here is his score:

Level 5 = Passed = 5.0
Level 6 = 2 errors = 0.0
Level 7 = 3 errors = 0.0
Level 8 = 9 errors = 0.0

Total Reading Estimate

5.0 Grade Level

An old group intelligence test score in his record showed that he had low average mental ability. We could expect him to read near the twelfth grade level had he finished high school. Instead he dropped out in the sixth grade where formal reading instruction had ended for him. He went to work after that and probably never had any reading instruction again. The sight vocabulary he had acquired was probably gleaned from context as he could not read these words accurately when seen out of context.

We know that remedial work has to begin at the fifth grade level and that the reading selections have to be of high motivational interest in order to entice James once again to take up reading instruction. His reversal of animal as "aminal" will make us investigate further the need for special training to overcome reversal tendencies in reading which would affect his reading speed and accuracy.

Remedial techniques and methods will be discussed in subsequent chapters. A list of words which are frequently reversed by older poor readers is given on page 62 of this chapter. The list can be used as a screening device.

3. Assessing Physical Factors

It goes without saying that anyone with any kind of a physical problem should be checked for causes of difficulties before any remedial work is started. Poor reading is no exception. We want to have some reasonable assurance that the person we are about to teach reading is "healthy" and that no ailment is interfering with his ability to read. A general physical examination by a competent physician will rule out most of our concerns. In some instances, eyesight, hearing, and neurological factors should be considered. Help should be sought only from competent professionals who are trained in their respective specialties.

Eyesight

If poor vision is suspected, an *optometrist* or *ophthalmologist* should be consulted. Even if nothing is wrong with the physical aspects of eyesight, the person still may have difficulties with visual perception; i.e., the way he perceives things. There is a difference between visual acuity (ability to see) and visual perception (way of seeing). Visual-perceptual training will be discussed in later chapters dealing with remediation.

The information that follows is contained in a flyer distributed by the National Society for the Prevention of Blindness, Inc., 79 Madison Avenue, New York, N.Y. 10016, and is reprinted here with the kind permission of the Society.

Signs of Eye Trouble in Children

Behavior

- Rubs eyes excessively.
- Shuts or covers one eye, tilts head or thrusts head forward.
- Has difficulty in reading or in other work requiring close use of the eyes.
- Blinks more than usual or is irritable when doing close work.
- Holds books close to eyes.
- Is unable to see distant things clearly.
- Squints eyelids together or frowns.

Appearance

- Crossed eyes.
- Red-rimmed, encrusted, or swollen eyelids.
- Inflamed or watery eyes.
- Recurring styes.

Complaints

- Eyes itch, burn, or feel scratchy.
- Cannot see well.

• Dizziness, headaches, or nausea following close eye work.
• Blurred or double vision.

OPHTHALMOLOGIST
OCULIST
OPTOMETRIST
OPTICIAN   . . . do you know the difference?

The following describes the qualifications of those providing eye health services: An *ophthalmologist* (oculist) is a doctor of medicine licensed to practice medicine and surgery who specializes in the diagnosis and treatment of diseases and defects of the eye by prescribing medicines, corrective lenses, and other types of treatment, including surgery.

An *optometrist* is a doctor of optometry licensed to practice optometry who specializes in the detection of defects of vision and treats them using corrective lenses and training.

A dispensing *optician* is one who fits, adjusts, and dispenses lenses, spectacles, eyeglasses, and other optical devices on the written prescription of a licensed physician or optometrist.

Hearing

In cases of poor hearing or suspected hearing difficulties, an *audiologist, otologist,* or *otolaryngologist* would have to be consulted to rule out hearing defects. The audiologist tests hearing acuity (ability) and can assess hearing loss by using audiometric (hearing measurement) devices. Again, he is concerned with the functional aspects of hearing, while the otologist is the medical specialist in this field who will try to discover damage to the hearing mechanisms, diagnose ear diseases, and prescribe necessary treatments. Since hearing is closely related to the sounds around us, a person having deficiencies in this area may have a hard time learning phonics (reading by ear).

Early detection and treatment are especially important in the correction of impaired hearing. The teacher or tutor can render invaluable help and service to students by observation and recognition of behavior or conditions which may indicate hearing difficulty. Here are some of the signs of suspected poor hearing:

- Lack of normal response to sound.
- Inattentiveness.
- Inability to follow oral directions.
- Failure to respond when spoken to.
- Frequent requests to have speaker repeat what he said.
- Intent observation of speaker's lips (lip reading).
- Habit of turning one ear toward a speaker.
- Unusual voice quality (e.g., monotonous).
- Speech too loud or too soft.
- Faulty pronunciation.
- Poor articulation.
- Frequent earaches or discharges from ears.

Coordination

Poor coordination, manifested in clumsiness while walking or playing on the yard, is another expression of some poor readers' physical condition. Gross motor and fine motor movements are related to reading ability and writing.

Among the medical specialists, the *neurologist* frequently is consulted if symptoms exist which may make one suspect neurological malfunctions. In some instances, medication has proven effective when prescribed by competent physicians. It is advisable to have a physician make the final decision for a referral to a neurologist or any other medical specialist since a layman can hardly be expected to recognize specific symptoms and what they might mean in terms of a neurological malfunction or disease. The neurologist also is the one who usually interprets the EEG (electroencephalogram), a brain-wave test.

Reversal Problems

Tendencies to reverse letters and words are frequently found in poor readers. This condition handicaps them in reading accurately and efficiently. Brief assessment of the type and extent of the problem can guide remediation efforts. For example, there are people who reverse "b" and "d" and thus introduce an error factor in their reading accuracy and fluency. Others reverse whole words, like "was" and "saw," or "stop" and "spot." As a routine check, a list of letters and words should be given to the student so that reversal tendencies can be observed and pinpointed. The letters and words contained in the list that follows were chosen because of their suggestiveness for reversals. They are "trap" words for the poor reader.

While no quantitative evaluation is attempted here, frequent reversals may tell the teacher that there is a condition which is in need of remediation. Exercises for this purpose will be found in later chapters dealing with remedial aspects of poor reading.

Words Provoking Reversal Tendencies

A. *Single Letters*

b   p   d   n   q   u   m   w   g

B. *Simple Words*

dab	tip	pal	pot	bad	did	bat	top	no
tub	was	on	saw	peek	doom	yam	pool	lap
loop	tend	dent	pin	raw	tend	bib	war	team

C. *Complex Words*
   (Errors of Transposition)

felt	wolf	pilot	flow	left	clover	blot
bolt	spaghetti	rift	cleft	crest	cringe	spastic
tilt	gripe	brats	smelter	alcove	plot	elastic
cliff	statistical	episcopal	clue	urgent	scalpel	pelt

4. Assessing Background Information

There is certainly more to the assessment of a reading problem than checking the reading level or finding indications of the intelligence level. However, this book is primarily concerned with a self-help approach; that is, immediate intervention by concerned adults around the poor reader. These people may be parents, brothers and sisters, relatives, neighbors, or professional teachers.

One cannot pull a student out of a slum area in the city in order to improve his reading. Or, it might not be possible to attack a father's drinking problem directly, although either of these factors might affect a child's ability to learn. The concept of "self-help" implies help with the problem where it exists. Massive intervention is another matter, one that we will not address here.

Most likely the poor reader we are talking about in this connection is still in a school situation having a hard time meeting success and avoiding failure. He may have dropped out of school already, finding himself in a quandary, or he may be a young adult working on a job but with little hope for advancement and job satisfaction because of his reading deficiency. Be that as it may, he needs help.

Using Specialists

There are many specialists in our schools and communities to whom an appeal for help may be directed. There are many adjunct and ancillary services which only recently have come to the fore and can be utilized to aid the person with learning problems, either directly or indirectly. Knowledge of existing persons and facilities in the community can be an added factor in remediation. For example, there are Learning Specialists who have specific knowledge in the field of learning disabilities. In schools, they are often found under such names as Reading Teacher, Reading Specialist, Resource Teacher, Language Specialist, Language Therapist, or Teacher of the Dyslexic. Other specialists in this array of helpers are the Occupational Therapist, Physical Therapist, Social Worker, and Community Coordinator. Still others are Public Health Nurse, Welfare Worker, and Rehabilitation Counselor. They all can help.

The more these professionals work as a team, the more they can bring their specialized knowledge to bear on an individual case and help the poor reader overcome his learning problem. For example, a physical education instructor can help a person with coordination exercises, while a social worker may be able to explore home conditions and make suggestions for improvements, or help others to accept a student's emotional reactions to his reading problem. But they must all work together as a team.

Perhaps a word of caution should be offered here. Specialists are professional people who require a state license in order to practice. A license protects the general public from unqualified practitioners. Licensing laws differ from state to state.

Emotional Problems

Emotional maladjustment sometimes occurs in connection with poor reading. Emotional maladjustment may be primary, in response to certain stress factors in life, or it may be secondary, as a reaction to continued failures and frustrations such as those encountered by poor readers. Emotional health and illness are the domain of the *psychiatrist* and *psychologist.* Here again we have some overlapping professional services and the proper choice of specialist may prove difficult to make. The psychiatrist is usually concerned with mental illness and is a medical specialist who can prescribe medication if indicated.

Figure 2-4A

Drawing by a 14-year-old male, eighth grade, IQ 104, reading on the sixth grade level. Drawing is suggestive of a poor self-image.

A

Figure 2-4B

Drawing by a 14-year-old male, IQ 107, eighth grade, reading on the late fourth grade level with numerous reversals in his reading. Note aggressive stance suggestive of a secondary emotional reaction to his learning problem.

B

The psychologist conducts evaluations assessing intelligence and achievement level, aspects of personality and emotional adjustment, and certain perceptual functions. He may also offer services in counseling and therapy, and, when specializing in this area, can be very helpful with learning disabilities such as poor reading.

What is primarily affected in the poor reader is his self-image. He feels defeated after having met with failure each time he tried to tackle the task of reading. He has not

Figure 2-4C

Drawing by 16-year-old male, grade 9, IQ 94, with auditory dyslexia, reading on the fifth grade level. Note details on head of human figure but lack of detail in the rest of the body. There is a lag of maturational development.

experienced the kind of success others have in simple tasks such as reading the newspaper with ease or getting good grades in school. Usually, the self-image improves when remediation is begun.

The drawings of a human figure in Figure 2-4, A-E, illustrate some of the frustrations expressed by poor readers. Human figure drawing is not suggested here as an assessment instrument for the layman, but is offered simply as a reflection of feelings, self-image, and inability to conceptualize the human figure. The drawings speak for themselves.

Figure 2-4D

Drawing by 13-year-old boy, grade 8, IQ 125, reading on the late sixth grade level. His special problem is dysgraphia (handwriting). Note interrupted line drawing suggestive of feelings of insecurity.

D

Vocational Interests

Vocational interests are important in the assessment procedure because they may reveal hidden interests and talents which can be used in the remedial approach. The poor readers we are talking about here are adolescents and young adults. They will have difficulties accepting texts which tell about a dog named Spot or a ride on a train. It would be better to let them read about how to train dogs or mechanical aspects of train engines. But books of this nature are still scarce, especially when they have to be written on a low reading grade level.

Figure 2-4E

**Drawing by an 18-year-old male, IQ 98, grade 11, reading on
the sixth grade level. His learning problem has a diagnosed
organic basis. Note the lack of a body concept (poor body
image) characteristic for this type
of poor reader.**

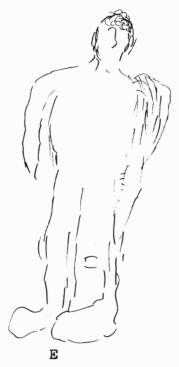

E

    One way of finding out about a person's interest is by
talking to him. A brief interview may bring out a person's
hobbies, experiences on past jobs, or desires for his vocational
future. These interests may then be related to choices of reading
materials.

    There are other ways of finding out about a person's
vocational interest. Perhaps a list of jobs can be given to the
poor reader (or read to him) and he can mark the careers he is
particularly interested in. Often his interests cluster around

certain jobs which are related, such as mechanics or managerial positions. At any rate, the assessment in this connection is informal, as opposed to more formal vocational interest inventories given by school counselors. The student's school records may contain valuable information which can guide the assessor.

THE PROFILE CHART: COMBINING ASSESSMENT DATA

In order to combine all assessment data and chart them on a simple summary profile, a form as shown in Figure 2-5 can be used.

Figure 2-5

Profile Chart

NAME__Charles Smith__ DATE OF BIRTH__9-4-58__ AGE__17__ DATE__9-17__

SCHOOL__Butler HS__ GRADE__11__ TEACHER OR COUNSELOR__T.M. Waller__

_____

I. INTELLIGENCE LEVEL

Group Test (Otis) IQ 102 (average) WAIS Full Scale 109 (adm. July 73)

II. READING LEVEL

WRAT Reading Grade 5.6 (in 8th Grade)
Reading Estimate 7.5 (Nov.10)
Recognizes words involving car parts.

III. PHYSICAL FACTORS

High fever at age 3 (105°F)
Many allergies
Last physical was OK
High number of reversal errors and transpositions (title for tilt)

IV. BACKGROUND INFORMATION (Educational, Social, Emotional, Vocational)

Frequent tardiness; high distractibility
Wants to become a mechanic

Figure 2-5 (cont'd.)

V. FINAL ASSESSMENT

Average ability. Reading approx. 3-4 grades below expectancy. Tendency to reverse words. Refer to Resource Teacher for further analysis of reading deficiencies.

VI. RECOMMENDED FOLLOW-UP

1. Placement in Remedial Reading class
2. Tutor for summer
3. Parent conference
4. Discuss in Team Meeting with all teachers

VII. INSTRUCTIONAL RECOMMENDATIONS

1. Increase motivation by using texts involving mechanical terminology
2. Stress reversal training
3. Develop sight vocabulary
4. Allow to give book reports orally
5. Encourage reading with mother at home, 20 min. per night

VIII. REMARKS

Re-evaluate before return in fall (12th Grade)

The data to be shown on the profile chart should summarize the teacher's own assessment. However, the profile may also include information from group-administered tests or outside sources. While teachers ordinarily do not administer and evaluate professional tests such as the Wechsler Intelligence Scales (WISC and WAIS), the results are frequently available in a narrative form and should be included as additional background information or verification of cruder assessment data. Information gleaned from interviews with students and their parents, or classroom observations and incidental yet relevant materials, also can be recorded. For example, it may be known that the father had a severe reading problem while in school, or that a number of siblings in the family did not go beyond the eighth grade in school.

Background information may be subdivided into educational, social, emotional, and vocational information, but the purpose of the profile sheet is to synthesize and summarize.

Another even more important aspect of the profile is the fact that we are dealing here with a self-help approach to remediation, in the absence of expensive remedial clinics or inaccessible and unavailable specialists. Their help can only be sought if they are within reach of an individual. If they are not, we cannot stand idly by while a poor reader suffers disadvantages and meets constant failure.

Chapter Summary

In order to help a person overcome his reading handicap, one must first make a rough survey to screen for levels of competencies and deficiencies. While the use of the word "screening" implies that the initial evaluations must be relatively brief and rough, a first investigation into the problem areas of poor reading encompasses several broad areas. Among these areas are level of intelligence (ability, both functional and potential), physical factors and related problems, reading level, and background information such as emotional adjustment or orientation in space, especially reversal errors. Other background factors may be secured through interviews with student and parents. Still more resources for background data are group test results or evaluations by outside agencies in the community. The teacher uses simple assessment procedures to gain a first impression of the scope of deficiencies but is primarily concerned with the behavioral level; that is, events and acts which can be observed rather than inferred.

Chapter 2 provides the teacher with some simple procedures, such as estimates and inventories, which help her in obtaining a first impression of the scope and severity of the reading problem. Poor readers often show a significant gap between actual reading level and their current grade placement or expectancy by age and intelligence level. Vocational interests, hobbies, family background, or a rough assessment of the self-image can be additional factors of value in this assessment. Further studies by professional workers may have to be done to find causative factors or more specific deficits. A simple profile can be used to summarize the findings and chart a course for effective remediation.

3

Establishing
a Good
Tutorial Relationship

From among the many teaching strategies and techniques at our disposal today, the so-called "tutorial approach," also known as the one-to-one relationship, has proven to be highly successful in remediating reading problems of a more severe nature. At first glance, the success of this tutor-student relationship seems obvious because the tutor does not have to cope with a classroom of 30 or even 40 students. Interruptions are kept to a minimum and concentration can take place in a controlled environment. But this is not the whole secret of the tutorial relationship. In fact, the physical aspects of the situation are not as important as the human or psychological aspects that enter into this relationship. Once improvement in reading can be demonstrated in a one-to-one tutorial situation, progression can proceed along these lines by forming small groups of poor readers. In small groups, the student still benefits from personal interactions with the tutor while making the instruction economically more feasible.

PREREQUISITES FOR THE TUTORIAL ROLE

Many kinds of people serve in the role of a tutor. There are professional teachers and untrained volunteers frequently working side by side. While in some instances a tutor may employ very specific remedial methods and techniques, there are situations in which "anything will do" to help the student. Apart from the professional vs. layman issue, or specific methodology vs. eclectic approaches, what are some of the characteristics all tutors should possess in order to carry out their important role?

1. *Genuine Interest*

   The tutor must be genuinely interested in the student he teaches. He must unselfishly give of himself without regard to monetary rewards. His intense concern for the student's problem guides him in his relationship with the student. He realizes that praise works better than punishment. He respects the fact that people can have problems; he has a firm belief that, through remedial intervention, improvement will be forthcoming.

2. *Love of Teaching*

   The tutor must love the type of work he is doing, and must do it without grudge or selfish motives. There are many people who have a natural "knack" for teaching, be they professional teachers or laymen recruited from the community at large. If teaching or tutoring is considered a chore or a burden, no success can be expected.

3. *Personal Involvement*

   Since older poor readers often have secondary emotional problems concomitant with their reading deficiencies, the tutor must become involved personally in the tutorial situation. Teaching "techniques" are not enough. Human concern and warmth are basic ingredients to penetrate the deeper psychological feelings of a disabled reader.

4. *Willingness to Learn*

A tutor must constantly search for new approaches and methods and be willing to participate in training programs with a mind open to new and innovative techniques. No one approach can be considered the "right" way. Teacher or tutor must learn from experience and continuously train himself in new ways of teaching. Both professional teachers and laymen need this constant upgrading of their skills.

5. *Responsibility*

While the tutor is responsible for the quality of work involved during tutorial sessions, he receives his instructions and general strategy of approach from a professional person. The tutor's primary function is to carry out these educational and professional prescriptions. He does not make incisive changes without professional consultation.

AN ANALYSIS OF THE TUTORIAL RELATIONSHIP

A tutor may be a highly qualified professional teacher with a Master's Degree, a retired schoolma'm, a college student, or anyone willing to take on the job. Because of this wide range of qualifications, one may sometimes wonder if it is not the relationship that appears to be the basic remediating agent or process, rather than only the teaching technique employed.

The nature of the tutorial relationship can be seen as a form of counseling or psychotherapy where human interactions are primary. Appropriate instruction becomes either a part of such relationship or is only of secondary importance (as a by-product of the relationship), depending on the extent of the reading problem and the reader's own emotional reaction to his problem. Formerly, the terms bibliotherapy and academic therapy were used, but neither one is in vogue any longer even though they do stress the therapeutic aspect of the remedial process. If expertise in methodology were the primary factor, how could it be then that an inexperienced teacher, a grandmother, a teenager, or an aide in school can help the student with his reading, and very often with great success? Of course, it cannot be denied that these tutors often work under the supervision of trained teachers, but the fact remains that these supervisors are usually not present during the tutorial sessions. Some people, on the other hand, claim that the improved human relationship in tutorial sessions is brought about by employing individualized and more appropriate teaching techniques.

Examination of this tutorial relationship requires a closer look at the interpersonal process between tutor/teacher and poor reader. It is quite obvious that the "normal" reader did not use or need this one-to-one relationship in order to acquire reading skills. A similar relationship exists with regard to counseling techniques where various schools or disciplines claim the field of counseling and report successful outcomes irrespective of the method employed by the counselor. Reading methods likewise are known to overlap. If a visual perceptual approach is indicated, methods such as Fernald's multi-sensory approach, Maria Montessori's perceptual-motor approach, or Frostig's visual-motor exercises strongly overlap. In the same way, when various counseling techniques are differentiated from one another, success for any specific approach is far from being proven. Whether the counselor is an adherent of Freud, Adler, Jung, Rogers, or Berne makes no difference: they all have reported success stories. While failures are less often reported, they are nevertheless implied in the technique. Much depends on the technique employed, but much more depends on the person who uses it. And even if two people use the same technique, the outcomes may differ markedly.

With reading methods being relatively non-specific in regard to the successful outcome, we must be careful not to gather all of our techniques in one basket. If tutoring as well as counseling depend so much on the choice and presence of a human being rather than on technique, we must search now for the underlying force or forces which apparently do the trick in tutorial remediation, at least as an adjunct to the overall remedial approach.

In the past we have apparently focused too intensely on the teacher as the imparting agent of knowledge, and the student as the often passive recipient of the knowledge. Much less is known about the "process," the fluid interchange and interaction between teacher and student. So, the search for the interpersonal construct is for what mediates between tutor and student. Their relationship is a warm, close, understanding, sympathetic, empathetic, and confidential one. We are dealing with the *affective* level of teaching, not the cognitive one. This cognitive or skill level might be taken over by teaching machines, at least in part, but no one has yet invented a machine that substitutes for a friendly tutor.

A SIMPLE MODEL

In order to arrive at a model from which the tutorial relationship can be derived, we might summarize the tutorial process and relationship in simple behavioral terms:

1. The poor reader has been exposed to conventional methods of reading but did not acquire the reading process successfully. These instructions were given in group situations.

2. In due time our poor reader developed secondary emotional reactions to his primary learning problem and exposure to continuous failures. He is beginning to be considered a "behavior problem."

3. When finally engaged in a tutorial relationship, where the setting is unique and individualized, he begins to show signs of progress.

4. The student gets feedback from the tutor regarding his abilities and disabilities. He also becomes engaged in interpersonal relations by discussing attitudes and feelings with the tutor. He is allowed to ventilate his emotions. He is no longer receiving constant criticism.

5. The student is taught in *two domains* at the same time; namely, on the academic/cognitive and the affective/emotional level.

6. As the student gains in academic growth and personal adjustment, he reaches acceptable levels of reading performance

and begins to be absorbed by the regular classroom situation. He is being "mainstreamed" again.

The preceding observations can be conveniently incorporated into a simple model shown in Figure 3-1. At the top of the graphic representation of the tutorial situation is the affective level where both tutor and student arrive at the merger of the self-image. The student generates his own self-image while the tutor modifies it by feedback. On the behavioral level, the following verbal exchange might take place between tutor and student (see next page):

Figure 3-1

Affective Level

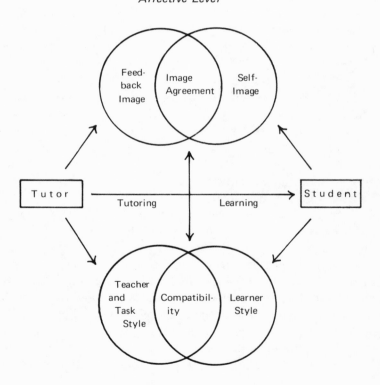

Cognitive or Skill Level

TUTOR: Well, let's try it!

STUDENT: I can't. Too hard. I just haven't got what it takes.

TUTOR: Come on, John, you did it yesterday. Try it again.

STUDENT: Well, OK. I'll try again; maybe this time I'll get it.

TUTOR: See, you can do it! Do it once more, come on!

STUDENT: Hey, I didn't know I could do that!

The lower level of Figure 3-1 shows the cognitive or skill level. Here straight teaching takes place but our poor reader still has to be taught with unconventional approaches and methods. The tutor has observed the learner's own learning style and now carefully selects the reading tasks that are *compatible* with his style and appropriate to the task. Again, as an example, let us tune in on a verbal interchange between tutor and student:

TUTOR: Well, how about reading this passage?

STUDENT: OK, but I have to do it my way.

TUTOR: That's fine with me. I know you like to look at the big words first and see if you can find some syllables that look familiar to you.

STUDENT: Well, let's see. There is *con,* that's a prefix, as you call it. Oh, here is *ion* at the end of the word. Don't tell me, let me figure it out by myself.

TUTOR: Go ahead!

STUDENT: Hey, con-ver-sation, that's it, *conversation.* I got it.

TUTOR: That was smart, John. Just break those big words down if you can't get them at first glance. Other students do it differently, like "sounding them out," you know. That's another way of doing it. We'll try that some other time, but meanwhile, keep on doing it your way. You read the word correctly: *Conversation.* Good, man!

The tutor does not switch systematically from cognitive to affective domain, but he may switch as the situation demands. He should not feel guilty if at any time during the session the student seems to need extended time on the affective level, especially in the beginning of the tutorial relationship. As the hurt self-image is built up, more and more work will be accomplished on the straight teaching, or cognitive/skill level.

TYPES OF TUTORIAL COUNSELING

Tutorial relationships exist in various forms and situations. If an emotional bond exists between tutor and student beforehand, such as that between mothers and their own sons and daughters, another look may have to be taken. Usually, but not always, the emotional closeness in family relationships is a deterrent to a healthy and free interaction between two people in a more formal instructional setting.

1. *Pal Tutoring.* This is a form of Buddy System where one student teaches his classmate or someone less proficient in reading than he is. For example, in some schools sixth graders are asked to tutor second or third graders on an individual basis for a brief period of the day. This practice boosts the ego of the sixth graders and benefits the second graders. Improvements in reading are usually reported for both the tutors and their pals.

2. *Parental Tutoring.* Fathers and mothers are usually poorly qualified as tutors for their own children because of the emotional closeness of the situation. In some instances, however, parents are able to detach themselves from the close situation and become effective tutors. It is advisable that in those instances the sessions are kept brief and businesslike. A reward system can reinforce the effectiveness of the sessions; e.g., receiving points or tokens after each successful session or completed task. These tokens may later be exchanged for something the student wants.

3. *Filial Tutoring.* Brothers and sisters in a family can serve as tutors for their younger siblings provided they have minimal maturity and a good relationship. Teenage youngsters often take a "Save little brother!" attitude which is admirable, but they also may need some guidance and advice from behind the scenes.

4. *Volunteer Tutoring.* Volunteer tutors make up by far the largest group of tutors. They are found in organized programs and special education classes. Frequently, these tutors are members of local organizations, such as Women's Clubs or college-based fraternities and sororities, who have become interested in tutoring as a club project. Their tutorial work is often confined to taking over segments of the regular teacher's work, such as short drills and programmed exercises.

5. *Teacher Tutoring.* By teacher tutoring is meant the teaching of reading to individual students by teachers whose major subject is not reading. For example, a biology teacher or physical education instructor may be made aware of a specific student's reading needs: The biology teacher could stress key words of his subject matter during regular classroom instructions and practice these words with the student by writing them on flash cards. The PE instructor can also help tremendously with perceptual-motor development and spatial orientation, important ingredients of the reading process on basic levels, by assigning special exercises to the student in need of such training. Left-right discrimination tasks, for example, are very helpful. Brief orientation sessions for these auxiliary reading tutors may be necessary to sensitize them to their new and often foreign task. These teachers also may not be fully aware of the relatively close relationship between their own subject matter and reading. In-service sessions should be conducted by experienced reading teachers and specialized consultants.

6. *Professional Tutoring.* The terms Professional Tutoring and Tutorial Counseling are reserved for trained specialists and may be carried out by remedial reading teachers and reading specialists who use a clinically oriented approach, or by high school counselors, rehabilitation counselors, and psychologists who have some professional background in counseling. In some

rare instances, psychiatrists have initiated tutorial therapy when they realized that their patients' emotional symptoms were secondary to a primary learning problem and therapy would be more realistic in this connection. These secondary emotional reactions may be reflected in a variety of symptoms; e.g., defense mechanisms, behavior disorders, or complete withdrawal.

7. *Small Group Counseling.* If groups are kept extremely small, like two to four adolescents per group, tutorial counseling may still be possible and is certainly more economical in time and investment. These tutorial sessions usually deviate somewhat from individual sessions since the approach involves group interaction. However, instructions may be programmed to cater to individual needs. Perhaps tasks specific to each participant can be assigned to individuals, while the emotive/affective segment of the tutoring can be done in groups.

8. *The Tutorial Counseling Pool.* In cases where suitable tutors cannot be located, blocks or entire neighborhoods can organize tutorial pools similar to babysitting services or car pools. Participating adolescents and their parent tutors are matched as closely as possible for congeniality. For example, in this "swap shop" approach a mother might feel that she cannot tutor her rebellious son, but she might select someone else's son in the neighborhood and swap him for her own. In this way, emotional balance is obtained and tutoring can proceed on calmer seas. This approach takes some leadership or organizational ability within the neighborhood.

Tutorial counseling as a technique seems particularly suited to adolescent youths and young adults when help with their reading problems is scarce or unavailable. When available, the price for tutoring is often high and not within reach of the ordinary citizen. Another reason why tutorial counseling can be effective, aside from the economy and efficiency of the approach, is the fact that the secondary emotional reactions in adolescents and young adults have often gone untreated and by now have become intensified. In some instances, the emotional aspects of a reading problem have to receive priority attention before the actual reading skills can be considered for remediation.

The theoretical model as shown in Figure 3-1 is applicable to almost any tutorial situation enumerated above. Lay tutors would probably perform more appropriately on the counseling level of the process; some expertise might be required for the skill level even though a programmed approach is used. In that case, the task is clearly cut out for the tutor on a ready-made basis. However, when tutors get specific instructions—that is, by using programmed approaches such as ready-to-use sheets or exercises—there should be no problem in handling the tutorial situations when minimal training or experience is provided. If the learning problem has been diagnosed by a specialist in the field, it is feasible that the diagnosis be translated into a total remedial program, which, in turn, could be used to prescribe a step-by-step procedure for the tutorial aide. Some supervision is advisable in the beginning until tutoring is well under way and some positive achievement can be shown. With the scarcity of professional tutors, much will have to be done by ancillary personnel if these young people are ever to obtain assistance with their reading problems.

A RATING SHEET FOR SCHOOL ADJUSTMENT

In tutoring and counseling a poor reader, or any individual for that matter, it is often quite helpful to employ a simple and practical aid or supplementary device to map out the individual's weak and strong feelings about himself. It is not only an informal assessment of his self-image, but a basis from which to work and begin effective tutoring and counseling.

The Rating Sheet for School Adjustment, reproduced in Figure 3-2, was designed for just such a purpose. The student is simply asked to rate himself on the ten dimensions, on a scale ranging from 1 to 5, with 1 being the highest and 5 being the lowest rating. No formal scoring system is attempted.

An additional step in this procedure can be employed: Get either teachers, or parents, or both, to rate the student on the same rating scale. In this way, one can easily pinpoint agreement and disagreement between and among the raters. A student might think he is highly motivated while his teacher or parents do not agree. In other instances, a student may rate himself high on school achievement, but his grades are low and do not agree with the self-image of the student. This disparity would be a helpful basis for discussion and counseling. Why the disparity? Why does the student feel he is a high achiever when records indicate he performs on a low level? Why does he think he is "dumb" when results of intelligence tests show an I.Q. of 120?

If ratings are obtained from three different sources—e.g., student, counselor, and parent—results may be entered on the rating scale with different-colored pencils for better visibility of differences or disparities. Overlaps of ratings mean agreement (and probably no problem), while wide gaps in ratings (2 or 3 points) spell disagreement (and possible problem areas).

Figure 3-2

Rating Sheet for School Adjustment

Rate yourself on a 5-point scale by placing a check-mark (✓) on top of the line over the appropriate number. Value of numbers: 1. Very much; 2. Much; 3. Average; 4. Not too much; 5. Very little or low. In case of indecision, the check-mark may also be placed between two numbers.

	1	2	3	4	5
I. *General Intelligence* How smart are you?					
II. *School Achievement* How well are you doing in school?					
III. *School Adjustment* How well are you getting along with teachers? Do you like school?					
IV. *Social Adjustment* How well are you getting along with your peers and grown-ups?					
V. *Parent Relations* How well are you getting along with your parents?					

Figure 3-2 (cont'd.)

VI. *Physical Health*

    What do you think about your
    health?

VII. *Emotional Adjustment*

    How well do you think you have
    yourself under control?

VIII. *Study Habits*

    What about your efficiency, tar-
    diness, getting up late, order-
    liness, homework, use of li-
    brary, reading of assignments?

IX. *Motivation*

    Are you interested and eager to
    do things in school?

    Do you feel a need or urge for
    achievement?

X. *Activity Level*

    Do you have lots of energy? Are
    you a go-getter? On the go?
    Fast?

Remarks:

NAME OF STUDENT: _____

                       Last   First

BIRTH DATE: _____ GRADE: _____

SEX: _____ COUNSELOR: _____

Chapter Summary

Tutoring proceeds on academic skill levels for purposes of remediating deficient reading performance. Effective tutoring is done on a one-to-one basis, which assures a warm and confidential setting and close interpersonal relationship. While professional teachers as well as laymen may serve in the role of a tutor, little is known about the relationship between *tutor and student. The chapter first discusses the role of the tutor with regard to essential characteristics a tutor must bring to the role. It then proceeds to analyze critically the essential features of the relationship and proposes a workable model. An actual verbal exchange between tutor and student is cited to illustrate what is going on during a tutorial session. Finally, a list of types of tutorial counseling is presented showing the variety of tutorial resources in both individual and group arrangements, followed by a simple and practical Rating Sheet as a helpful counseling aid.*

One of the most important aspects of the tutorial relationship must be sought in the dual level approach which the intimate relationship entails. The tutor integrates an academic and affective level of tutoring as needed, thus providing academic as well as emotional support to the poor reader. Older poor readers are in dire need of the affective support. Their low academic performance has been overlooked in the past and often has caused the reader to withdraw or otherwise react negatively to the continuous chain of failures.

4

Choosing
Basic Approaches
to Remediation

This chapter describes basic approaches to reading, with specific reference to specialized methods for dealing with older poor readers. When selecting special techniques, a veritable smorgasbord of gimmicks, techniques, methods, and materials is available to the teacher. This statement may be as helpful as it is confusing to the teacher. There is no single, unique way of teaching reading. A general guideline to the teacher is that whatever method, or combination of methods, *works* for an individual teacher and his student *is the right method.* Positive feedback—i.e., the student's improvement in his reading—is the best way of finding out about a certain method. In a more refined way, this method is known as "Diagnostic Teaching."

In a very basic sense, there have been two approaches to reading over the past years; namely, the sight and the sound approaches, or the phonetic and visual methods. During the past decade, however, new approaches have made themselves known, often variations of older ones or those based on scientific and linguistic research. In the phonetic approach, the child is taught the sound value of each letter or letter combination of the alphabet. Since the English language roughly is only 70 percent phonetic—i.e., follows phonetic rules—the method obviously has its drawbacks. How are we going to recognize the remaining 30 percent of the words for which we have no phonetic clues? The letter C can be pronounced like "K" as in *cream,* or like a voiceless "S" as in *citrus.* It is obvious that there is no phonetic difference in the words *see* and *sea,* both sounding out a "long e." "Fonetic Phanatics" will have a hard time explaining these difficulties!

The second approach is the purely visual, or sight word approach. Here the student learns the words, and later the whole sentence, by recognizing the configuration of the word or sentence structure, without going into phonetic analysis at all. The word *cat* is presented and learned as one whole unit or Gestalt, not the combination and agglutination of three separate sound symbols. In this way, students are required to develop a "sight vocabulary," ranging from simple words like *cat* to more difficult ones like *refrigerator.* Illustrations in the textbook or primer are supposed to help the student with associating pictures and words, assuming (hopefully!) that he may later on recognize the word without its pictorial referent. Many a student became a "word guesser" in this way, and gradually, a "poor reader."

Which one of these two approaches is the better, or the preferred one? Neither, according to the experts. An improved product can be obtained by using both approaches simultaneously, or preferring one over the other according to the student's "cognitive style" as facilitating agent in the process of reading. Further advantages can be taken by inclusion of structural clues, oral language development, motivational utility words, or career-oriented texts.

THE SOUND APPROACH

Before attempting to teach by the phonetic approach, assurance must be obtained by the teacher that the student possesses good auditory discrimination. Some people simply are tone-deaf and do not respond readily to phonetics. In addition, many "older poor readers," who have been exposed again and again in their scholastic past to remedial phonics, but without success, simply cannot respond to this approach. It may prove to be a futile endeavor to start these young people once again on a method to which they failed to respond in the past. Phonics should then be taught on an *incidental* rather than systematic basis, or should receive less emphasis in the overall reading program.

Developing Auditory Discrimination and Memory

IMPORTANT: The exercises below should not be carried out over an extended period of time. In order to avoid motivational inertia, individual exercises should not exceed 15 minutes at a time.

A complete Quick Educational Prescription Finder can be located at the end of Chapter 5 for easy and ready reference to all exercises in Chapters 4 and 5.

The following exercises are recommended for developing auditory discrimination as a receptive as well as expressive part of the entire process. First, the student is trained to discriminate the message, then he is required to express it in three different ways: manually, nonverbally, and verbally. The stimuli likewise are varied by being presented both auditorily and visually, and are then converted by the student into the three aforegoing expressive modes. For this reason, the next exercise is broken down into several steps.

Exercise 4.1   *Can You Repeat These Signals?*
                                      (Beeps, Digits, Letters)

A material prerequisite for these exercises is a noise-making instrument to generate sound. The best way to do this is to have a telegraph key available, similar to the ones used with Morse Code (see Photo 4-1). However, a whistle, piano, or similar device will suffice. If these are unavailable, human voice may be used by simply saying "dot–dash–dot," or "short–long–short," or "beep–beeeep–beep." The idea is to present sound stimuli which the student can perceive auditorily. In addition to a sound source, 3 x 5 index cards are also needed for visual presentation of stimuli (see Figure 4-1, page 93).

Photo 4-1

**Use of the Telegraph Key and Cue Cards
in Auditory Training**

STEP I: Auditory Presentation—Manually expressed audible response

"Beep out" Morse Code type signals on the telegraph key, as follows:

$$\bullet\ \bullet\ - \qquad \text{(short, short, long)}$$
$$-\ \bullet\ -$$
$$\bullet\ \bullet\ -$$

Ask the student to repeat these signals by using another telegraph key. The exercise proceeds from simple to complex signals, according to the student's ability. If auditory deficit is severe, short signals must be given first and complexity built up gradually.

This is a *simple* signal: • •   or   — •

This is a *complex* signal: • • — • • •   or   — — • — • • —

The student is simply required to listen carefully and then reproduce the signal manually. He does not use speech in any form to reproduce the signals. In addition to auditory recall and discrimination, this exercise should improve auditory memory span.

STEP II: Auditory Presentation—Orally expressed response

In the same way as in STEP I, ask the student to repeat the signals given to him on a telegraph key. After perceiving the auditory signals, ask the student to repeat the signals, by giving them back to you orally; e.g., short-short-long, or dot-dot-dash, or beep, beep, beeeep.

STEP III: Auditory Presentation—Visual-motor response (written)

Again as in STEP I, beep out signals on the telegraph key, according to the student's ability. This time he must repeat the signals in writing, which requires him to have paper and pencil. As you beep out the signals, the student writes them down using dots and dashes as his symbol system:

Teacher signal: • • —   Student's written response: • • —

Through gradually increasing the length of the signals by adding dots and dashes, the exercises also improve memory span. STEPS, I, II, and III are now repeated but with *visually* presented stimuli.

STEP IV: Visual Presentation—Manually expressed response

Have 3 x 5 index cards prepared by writing Morse Code type signals on them with a black felt-tipped marker for clear visibility (see Figure 4-1A). Hold up a card and show it to the student for a few seconds. The student is now required to perceive the stimulus visually but express it manually.

Teacher shows card with dots and dashes. = Student repeats signal on card by beeping it out on a telegraph key (non-verbally).

As in the STEPS above, the teacher gradually increases the complexity of the signals from short to longer codes. An increase in complexity of the signal means improving discriminatory powers, while an increase in the length of the signal means improving memory span. The same exercise can be done in the visual as well as the auditory realm of perception, depending on the student's needs and deficiencies.

STEP V: Visual Presentation—Orally expressed response

Again, present the visual stimulus cards as under STEP IV, above. Ask the student to repeat the signals shown, but this time let him *say* them, like "dot, dot, dash" or "short, short, long." Do *not* require the student to do any written work for this exercise.

Further variations in complexity and transfer of learning can be obtained by replacing dashes and dots with digits, letters, or words (see Figure 4-1,B).

For example:

Digits (series of numerals)
5 8 3 9 8
6 4 9 7 3 2 1

Letters of the alphabet
H F N E Z
K L R T P E

Words
bag — house — apple — fudge
bucket — grocery — picture — chair

Figure 4-1

**Visual Stimulus Card for
Auditory Training**

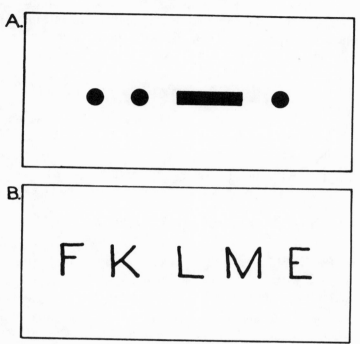

The variations above can be repeated orally and in writing. Another way to have the student reproduce these signals would be to give him a series of answer cards (two or three) and ask him to point to the correct answer card. However, this procedure would probably be more suitable for work with the hearing-impaired student than with regular poor readers.

Exercise 4.2 *Telephone Exchange*

Pretend you are the switchboard operator and ask the students to call each other. A student may "call" you by asking for another student's number, say 569-8774. Give the number to the caller by telling him the series of digits. He has to

repeat the number, and the called party has to answer by saying
"Yes, this is 569-8774." If the student cannot repeat the
number correctly, you say "Wrong number!" and give him the
correct number again. If seven digits should prove too difficult
to handle in the beginning, the phone numbers may be
shortened, to say 389 or 773, in order to make it similar to
house phone extensions.

Exercise 4.3   *Auditory Closure (Contextual Clues)*

Say a brief sentence and ask the student to fill in the blank
spot.
For instance, say:

The man with the blue (blank) is my father.
Here comes Charlie, who always (blank) when he greets
you.
When the car started to stall I knew it was (blank) that had
given out.

The student's ability to recall can also be improved by making
up sentences with blanks after a particular story has been read.
This exercise is strictly oral.

Remember Jessie Brown who always wore a (blank) shirt?
When Lillian looked out of the window she noticed a
(blank).
It was (blank) when Joe and his buddies returned to the
garage.

Phonetic Exercises

Exercise 4.4   *Initial and Medial Sounds*

This is a phonetic exercise for students having difficulty
with initial and medial sounds. Adolescents might sometimes be
embarrassed by the simplicity of the task and care must be
taken that the setting is sufficiently isolated and confidential to
avoid such reactions.

STEP I

Give the student a "sound" letter like "unvoiced B" and ask him to name other words which start with the same sound.

B bear, barber, booster, blotter, beefsteak, bamboo, beard.

F flee, fly, foster, father, feather, friend, folder.

STEP II

After the student has mastered the initial sounds, try a somewhat harder exercise. This time he must recognize middle (medial) sounds and give you more examples with the same middle sound.

F different, differ, puffing, sniffing, shifting, suffer, coffee, buffer.

G giggle, rigging, tiger, Niger, biggest, beggar, bugle.

Exercise 4.5   *Listening Comprehension*
(Reading by Exposure to Sound)

Record a small passage or story from a reader using a tape or cassette recorder. The text level must match the student's instructional or interest level. Give the student the printed text and ask him to listen to your recording while following the story in the book with his eyes. He may listen to it by earphone or loudspeaker. Do not ask him to read out loud as this might prove confusing and induce stuttering. Some comprehension questions may be asked later. You may want to prepare several passages on tape for a wider selection. Commercially produced tapes, cassettes, and phonograph records are also available.

Exercise 4.6   *The Phonetic Wheel*

This gadget-type exercise is appealing to students because they can manipulate it as they learn. Two students, checking each other's work, can use the wheel independently.

Construct the Phonetic Wheel by cutting out a disc from a sheet of cardboard. Figure 4-2 (page 97) will help you to visualize the final product. Two circular cut-outs are needed, one somewhat larger than the other, with the smaller one being on top of the larger one. Fasten the circles together with a paper fastener so that the top wheel can be turned by the student. The outer edge of the large wheel has initial consonants, while phonograms are written on the smaller disc. The student now aligns the initial consonants and the phonograms to form new words.

Since not all initial consonants are suitable for making words with the word endings, the student must select only those words which make sense. Initial consonants must be sounded out by the student, otherwise the task is not phonetic but visual in nature. Sample phonograms for the bottom wheel are given below.

amp	ill	art	oes
ear	one	ove	oll
eep	oor	on't	ead
ip	ump	ate	ell

Here are examples of words which can be dialed on the Phonetic Wheel:

d-amp	l-amp	r-amp	c-amp	
d-oor	t-one	p-art	c-art	t-art

Exercise 4.7   *Fill in the Blank*

Sometimes the student possesses a fair reading vocabulary but needs reinforcement to strengthen phonetic and visual memory. Present the student with a list of words he already knows. Leave out certain parts, such as a letter (consonants and vowels, singly and in clusters). The student is required to fill in the blanks, saying the words aloud as he does the exercise.

Examples:

Vowels	n . . dle	(needle or noodle)
	p . nc . l	(pencil)
	r . bber b . nd	(rubber band)

Figure 4-2

Sample of a Phonetic Wheel

Large Disc:
Outer Disc
on Bottom

Turn

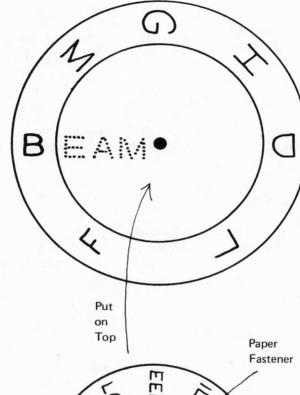

Put
on
Top

Paper
Fastener

Small Disc:
Inner Disc
on Top

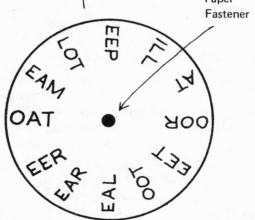

Consonants	mi . er	(mixer, miner, miler, miser)
	go . d	(gold)
	pira . e	(pirate)
Consonantal Clusters	. . otter	(blotter, trotter, clotter, spotter)
	ta . .	(task, tack, tank, talk, tall)
	pu . . it	(pulpit)

The words suggested in the exercise should be within reach of the student's ability in order to prevent the exercise from becoming a word guessing game.

Exercise 4.8   *Phonetic Starters*

Place several small cardboard boxes in front of the student. Give him a stack of previously prepared index cards. For example, the cards may have words written on them beginning with three different consonants: B, F, and R. In this case, ask the student to place all of the cards into three boxes marked with the appropriate letters. (Small paper bags can be used instead of the boxes.) Here are some sample words:

bag	fun	run
bean	finger	Randy
bolting	filing	rigging
basket	filter	Russia

Some confusion may exist regarding the same sound as differentiated from the same initial letter. For instance, words like *carburetor* and *karate* have the same initial sound but not the same initial letter. On the other hand, the words *city* and *cat* have the same initial letter but not the same initial sound! In this exercise, sound is to be stressed.

The exercise can be varied to fit the students' needs. Older students particularly need words taken from their environment or field of career interest. Instead of initial single sounds, medial or final positions can be chosen.

Exercise 4.9 *Choose a Sound*

Choose a sound as the initial, medial, or final consonant in a word, say B. Ask the students to name orally as many words as they can, with the B as the beginning, medial, or final position sound. Each student gets a turn and a time limit is set, maybe 30 seconds. The student who named the largest number of words is the winner. If a mistake is made, just don't count the word. No punishment in a tutorial setting!

Another version would be to name *vowel* sounds for the three positions and ask the student to rattle off their words, like "able, acorn, apes, etc." To avoid having a good student always the winner, the group can participate in pairs or teams. Small trinkets may be used to reinforce success.

These exercises represent a selective sample of activities in phonics and are not intended to be an exhaustive presentation. The references at the end of the book may lead the teacher to additional sources.

THE VISUAL APPROACH

Over 80 percent of what we learn we perceive through our visual sense. This should convince everyone that vision plays an important role not only in our lives in general, but especially in matters of reading. While the accuracy of vision is not of interest at this point, visual discrimination must be of concern. The importance of visual perception is further emphasized by the fact that the English language is approximately 70 percent phonetic, but the remaining 30 percent cannot be learned by simple phonetic drills. Here visual recognition must take over to help us with the irregularities of the language. But when we combine the phonetic and the visual approach, we have an even better chance to facilitate reading. In the next chapter, we shall see that even these two sensory modalities are often not sufficient to teach reading to older students who have traditionally been exposed to the audio-visual approach but have not fully benefited from it. Other sensory modalities have to be added.

Strengthening Visual Perceptions

There are many exercises a teacher or tutor can do with students to strengthen visual perception with regard to reading. However, it is important that the exercises selected appeal to older students who certainly have been exposed to this type of training in the past, in one form or another. "Childish" and silly exercises must be replaced by those which are motivational in nature and contain elements which the older student will find interesting and worth trying. Among this author's favorites is "Shoot the Cannon!"

Figure 4-3

The "Shoot the Cannon!" or "FIRE!" Game

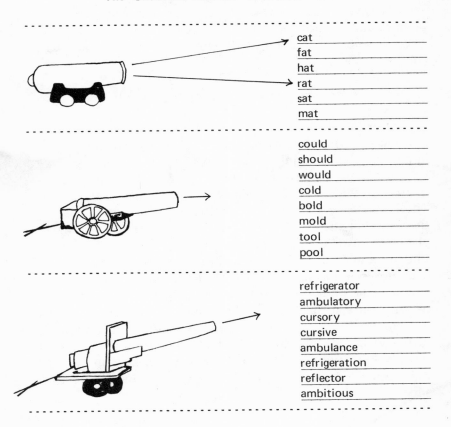

cat ___
fat ___
hat ___
rat ___
sat ___
mat ___

could ___
should ___
would ___
cold ___
bold ___
mold ___
tool ___
pool ___

refrigerator ___
ambulatory ___
cursory ___
cursive ___
ambulance ___
refrigeration ___
reflector ___
ambitious ___

Visual Perception Exercises

Exercise 4.10   *Shoot the Cannon!*

Prepare a stencil showing a cannon on the left side of the paper, and a column of lines in the right margin (see Figure 4-3). These lines are for the list of words which are the targets. Choose words which are under study or which might attract the student. The words serve as targets for the cannon. Now say "Shoot the cannon!", or simply "Fire!" At this command, the student puts the point of his pencil at the mouth of the cannon and takes aim, fixing his eyes on the list of words to the right. When the teacher says the word she wants to be shot down (e.g., Fire at *should!*), the student moves the pencil across the paper and "hits" the word. The teacher continues to call words until all words in the right column are shot down. New words can now replace the old ones. The exercise sharpens word recognition. It also is excellent for reinforcing left-right movements. If a less aggressive exercise is needed, the cannons may be replaced by the drawing of a boy/girl throwing a ball.

Exercise 4.11   *Hit the Word!*

A variation of Exercise 4.10, is the Hit the Word! game. The basic difference is that the student has a narrower choice of words in front of him and he is allowed more acting-out behavior.

Write three of four words, widely spaced, on the board. Choose words that are within the student's ability range. Ask him to stand away from the board and in front of the words. At your command of "Throw!" or "Hit the word!", he is allowed to throw a paper or "nerf" ball at the word which the teacher named. For instance, you might say "basketball" or "fishing." Photo 4-2 shows the chalkboard arrangement. Two or three students might be asked to compete with each other. Each hit counts 1 point. Each player may have five turns, as time permits. Reserve the exercise for a rainy day, or for the end of the period.

Photo 4-2

The "Hit the Word!" Game

Exercise 4.12   *Word Configurations*

It has been found that many poor readers do not perceive a word or sentence as a whole configuration, or Gestalt. Since the word consists of letters, the student must combine them visually to form a whole rather than focusing on single words. To facilitate the perception of "wholes," this exercise provides a frame for the word for quicker visual recognition.

In the beginning, ask the student to draw a line around a given word, or to box it in. After this, provide the boxes and let the student draw in the word. Figure 4-4 presents several examples.

Exercise 4.13   *Embedded Letter and Word Clusters*

This exercise is particularly helpful in strengthening the part of visual perception which deals with figure-ground relationships; i.e., lifting a part from the perceptual background into the foreground. It allows the student to concentrate on the segment of the word or phrase which is the perceptual fore-

Figure 4-4

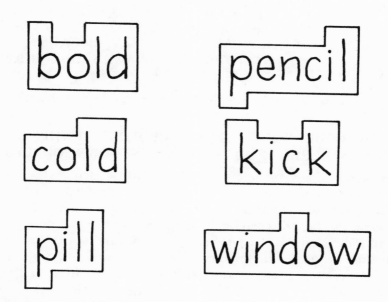

ground (the figure) against the perceptual background (the ground).

Ask the student to go over the following passages and let him encircle or underline the combination of successive letters which spell CAR within a word. This letter cluster may appear alone (car), or it can be found embedded in longer words (scar, cardiac).

Examples: SCARLET-COLORED CARS ARE SEL-
DOM DISCARDED IN GARAGES.

THE FARMER HAD A SCAR AND SAT IN A CART READING A CARD WHILE SITTING ON A CRATE.

Other exercises may call for the underlining of certain letter combinations.

Example: Underline the letter combinations "sk" and "sc" in the following passage:

THE BRISK WALK OF THE HUSKY RASCAL WAS RISKY BECAUSE HE STARTED TO SKIP AND SCOOT WHICH SCARED THE ESCAPEE.

Of course, other letter combinations can be introduced, such as "the" in:

THE OTHER THEME OF THE THEOLOGICAL THESIS WAS GATHERED FROM THUS FAR UNKNOWN SOURCES.

The exercise is very helpful, especially for students who have difficulty recognizing consonant clusters embedded in words, like scarce, scarlet, brisk, or Episcopal. Accuracy and speed in reading can be enhanced by doing this exercise more frequently with these students. Easy-to-read magazines and weekly readers provide a good source for these exercises. Just give the student or class a letter combination, like CAR, THE, or BUT, and let them underline the combination in the chosen text. The purpose is to make them focus on the most difficult part of the word and select it from the remaining part of the word. The passages should be prepared or selected in accordance with the person's reading level.

Using Flashcards and Tachistoscopic Devices

Word recognition exercises can be enhanced by making use of simple tachistoscopic devices which allow for quick exposures of words and phrases. While these devices are available commercially, they can be built at a much lower cost and serve the same purpose. They can be made from cardboard, with slots cut out for word exposure.

Exercise 4.14   *Flash Cards*

The simplest quick exposure device is the flash card. This is a time-proven method which must not be overlooked in remedial work. Index cards and a felt tip pen are all that is needed. Expose the cards one by one and ask the student to read the word on the card. Cards which he recognized immediately are placed in one pile, while cards which were difficult for him are placed in another pile for more frequent repetition.

In addition to using the flash card stacks for word drills, they can also be used to provide a record of student progress in word recognition. After the drill, count the number of cards that were not read with ease or where mistakes were made. After each drill, enter the number of correct words on a Progress Chart, along with the date, as shown in Figure 4-6. A simple flash card is shown in Figure 4-5, below.

Figure 4-5

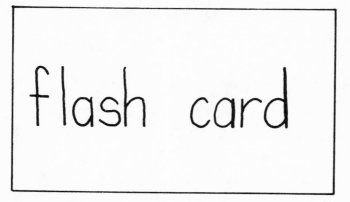

Exercise 4.15   *Simple Tachistoscopes*

The construction of a simple word exposure device, or home-made tachistoscope, is shown in Figure 4-7. A long piece of cardboard provides the basic construction. A narrow slot is cut to serve as the exposure window. Columns of words are now written on long strips of paper which fit through the slot. The words are taken from daily lessons and may precede actual reading of texts, or they may be used as review words to reinforce what has been learned. Two sample lists of words follow:

        bold   imagination
        block   invention

clock	convention
stock	exception
rock	reception
dock	friction
sock	conception
cold	eviction
roll	contraption
toll	conviction
told	addiction

Figure 4-6

Simple Progress Chart

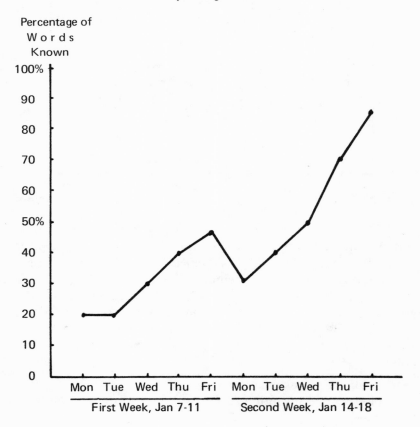

Figure 4-7

Home-Made Tachistoscope (Word Flasher)

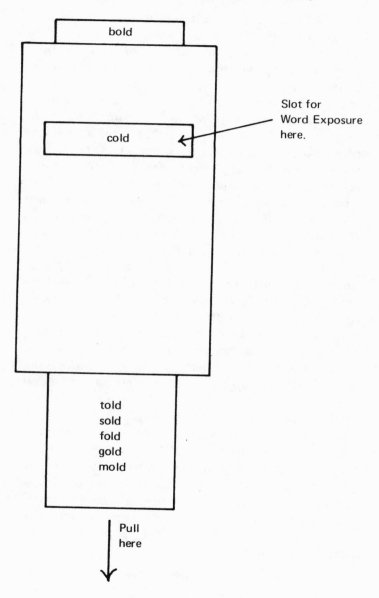

Chapter Summary

Choosing broad approaches to remediation must be based on the individual student's needs and deficiencies. A student who has a hard time discriminating between two sounds would not benefit from phonetic training or a phonetic approach to reading at first. Following basic auditory discrimination training, however, he may be ready for phonetic drills. There are two common approaches to the acquisition of reading: by sight and by sound. For the normal reader, these two approaches are most effective and successful when they are combined in the audio-visual approach. However, since the poor reader has not been able to benefit from such basic approaches in the teaching of reading, adjustments have to be made when remediating reading deficiencies.

This chapter provides the teacher with some proven methods and techniques to supplement instructions in the basic approaches to teaching reading. Students who have difficulty with phonics should be offered help in the strengthening of their discriminatory powers in listening. Words may have to be ·replaced with simple signals such as dots and dashes, the familiar symbols of the Morse Code. Students deficient in auditory discrimination need exercises which train them in both input and output avenues; i.e., receiving a message and expressing a message. They also need to be trained in combining the visual with the auditory for best results in reading. The exercises outlined in this chapter go beyond those found to be effective with "normal" readers. Since some poor readers need strengthening of their basic perceptual skills at a deeper level, the exercises focus heavily on these skills.

5

Selecting
Specific Remedial
Techniques

There are several ways in which one could classify remedial methods and techniques. Naming the author or originator of the method, like Montessori or Fernald, is one way. Another way to group these approaches might be by classifying them in terms of their common properties and methodological characteristics, like multi-sensory or programmed techniques. To simplify grouping the methods, the classification-by-characteristics system will be used in this chapter to make reading it more comprehensible for teachers and parents with little background in the teaching of reading.

Throughout the discussion of remedial techniques, the needs of older students will be kept in mind. Most older students who are poor readers have already been exposed to conventional reading instructions while attending elementary school. Educators must now find special (that is, more specific) methods which apply to students who are by now not only

109

highly skeptical about reading instruction but who have been turned off by the repeated failures implicit in ineffective methods and, consequently, in faulty learner responses. This is, indeed, a difficult task, challenging both the compassionate educator and the parent willing to try, try again.

Since older poor readers did not acquire reading skills in the conventional way, additional sensory avenues must be tapped when attempting to remediate their deficient skills. This is especially important for older students who read on a very low grade level (anywhere up to the fifth or sixth grade level), where the basic skills must be thoroughly mastered before they can go on to higher levels of reading skills.

At these lower levels of reading, the student has not mastered the basic skills and needs reinforcement in any way and via all sensory avenues available to him. Once the older poor reader is freed from the limiting chains of partial and underdeveloped skills, he can move on to higher levels. This is often a matter of practice and motivation where the challenge spurs the individual on to more reading, while experience and variety, in turn, improve and facilitate reading. Basic sensory skills can now give way to higher cognitive functions and reading speed (rate of reading) and comprehension can be developed. Once basic skills are mastered, the reader can also take advantage of contextual clues and conceptual inferences. The true freedom of reading has finally been attained.

As was described in Chapter 4, the two most common ways to teach reading are the phonetic and sight word approaches; that is, teaching reading via auditory and visual sensory avenues that lead to the brain. Or expressed in a simpler way, teaching reading is accomplished by using the eyes and ears. When both methods are combined for more effective acquisition of reading skills, it is commonly referred to as the Audio-Visual Approach to reading.

The fact still remains that some people do not benefit from ordinary classroom experiences and do not acquire the skill of reading in spite of instruction by the audio-visual approach. Somehow these people seem to be "wordblind" and/or "worddeaf" and cannot assimilate written symbols by ear and eye alone. They have normal intelligence and usually have nothing wrong organically, i.e. physically. These more

severe conditions of poor reading, found in young and old
people, are often referred to as dyslexia, a specific reading
disability. There are other labels used to describe this reading
problem. The skill of reading may be affected partially or
totally, ranging from slight to severe degrees of reading deficits.
People who do not master the skill of reading fully, may not
recognize or comprehend what they have only partially or
inaccurately read.

Table 5-1 provides an overview of existing remedial reading
methods. The table does not claim completeness because there
exists a multitude of methods today, often only slight variations
of more basic approaches. The entry for each method names its
outstanding proponent or originator and presents some examples of specific programs available from various sources. The
following section describes each of these methods in more detail
and should give the reader an orientation to the various
approaches to remedial reading and intervention techniques.

Table 5-1

Specific Remedial Reading Methods

Type of Method and Name of Representative, or Principal Exponents	References to Representative Programs and Resources
Multi-Sensory Grace Fernald Samuel Orton Maria Montessori	*Orton-Gillingham Method* Educators Publishing Service, Inc. 75 Moulton Street Cambridge, Mass. 02138 *VAKT Method* (Visual, Auditory, Kinesthetic, Tactile) McGraw-Hill Book Company, Inc. New York, N.Y.: Remedial Techniques in Basic School Subjects (G. Fernald)

Table 5-1 (cont'd.)

Type of Method and Name of Representative, or Principal Exponents	References to Representative Programs and Resources
Programmed B.F. Skinner M.W. Sullivan Myron Woolman	*Programmed Reading Series* C.D. Buchanan and Sullivan Associates McGraw-Hill Book Company, Inc. New York, N.Y. *Semi-Programmed Series* The Mott Basic Language Skills Program Allied Education Council P.O. Box 78 Galien, Mich. 49113
Impress (Neurological Impress) R.G. Heckelman H.C. Tien	*The Neurological Impress Method* Academic Therapy Publications San Rafael, California 94901: Solutions to Reading Problems (R.G. Heckelman) *The Ba-Be-Bi Method* Psychological Test Company East Lansing, Mich.: Reading by Inoculation with the AEIOU&Y Method (H.C. Tien, 1964)
Modified Alphabet or Spelling Sir James Pitman Caleb Gattegno	*i/t/a (Initial Teaching Alphabet)* Initial Teaching Alphabet Publications, New York, N.Y. Early-to-Read: i/t/a Program (Mazurkiewicz, A.J. and Tanzer, H.J., 1963)

Table 5-1 (cont'd.)

Words-in-Color
Learning Materials, Inc.
100 East Ohio Street
Chicago, Ill.

Structural-Linguistic
Leonard Bloomfield
Charles C. Fries
Catherine Stern

Bloomfield System
Clarence L. Barnhart, Inc.
Box 359
Bronxville, N.Y.

Fries Linguistic Readers
(A Basic Reading Series Developed Upon Linguistic Principles)
Fries Publications
Ann Arbor, Mich., or
Charles E. Merrill Books, Inc.
Columbus, Ohio

The Structural Reading Series
The L.W. Singer Company, Inc.
Syracuse, N.Y.
(Catherine Stern, 1963)

Phonetic
Rudolf Flesch
Schoolfield and
Timberlake

Phonetic Keys to Reading
The Economy Company
Oklahoma City, Okla.

Phonovisual Method
Phonovisual Products
Box 5625, Friendship Station
Washington, D.C.

Teaching Phonics with Success
Mafex Associates, Inc.
111 Barron Avenue
Johnstown, Pa. 15906
(R.F. Wagner, 1960)

SPECIAL TECHNIQUES AND METHODS

The Multi-Sensory Approach

The basic aim of the Multi-Sensory Approach is to retrain sensory modalities in addition to the visual and auditory, in order to help the student overcome his reading handicap. The more avenues leading to the brain, the surer the success of acquiring reading skills. Besides the visual and auditory, there are the tactile, olfactory, and kinesthetic senses, or put in simple language, feeling, smelling, and orientation in space. The anagram VAKT stands for visual, auditory, kinesthetic, and tactile.

A number of methods advocate the multi-sensory approach, either partially or totally. Among the more prominent methods are those developed by Grace Fernald in the United States, Maria Montessori in Italy, and Samuel Orton, the American neurologist. Orton's contributions are known methodologically as the Orton-Gillingham approach. Writing in 1943, Fernald found that her backward readers were unable to analyze words, and her now-widely-used kinesthetic method was designed to help these poor readers overcome their specific deficiencies. Montessori emphasized a basic perceptual approach beginning in very early childhood. Children traced the shapes of letters with their fingers on cut-out sandpaper letter forms, among other exercises.

Orton taught that a condition of mixed laterality (sidedness) of the two hemispheres of the brain might be the cause of many poor readers' dilemma, and he referred to the scrambled output of his patients' spelling and writing as "strephosymbolia," Greek for scrambled symbols. Together with Gillingham he developed a remedial method stressing a tactile-kinesthetic approach, using techniques such as writing letters and words in the air or on rough surfaces.

Many of the multi-sensory approaches today combine several techniques, such as tracing letters and simultaneously saying their phonic values as one sees the visual shape (letters).

The olfactory sense modality is the least stressed in all of these approaches, but some exercises may require smelling of pictures and words scented to evoke the meaning of the word. For example, a picture of a rose, or the word "rose," may actually have scented print and smell like a rose. At other times, little bottles may be labeled with the names of certain scents. The "reader" can open the bottle and identify by smell contents such as lemon, cocoa, or peppermint.

The Impress Method

In this rather simple but unique approach, the teacher/ tutor and the student read the text in unison; i.e., they sit side by side and read the text simultaneously aloud. No formal corrections or stops for explanations are made during the reading. The approach is particularly suited for older students because, by this age, the older poor reader has resigned from enthusiastic participation in any classroom exercises because corrections by the teacher have been embarrassing to him.

What is so unique about the method is its simplicity and straightforwardness. Feedback is given in a very subtle way: instead of being corrected constantly, the student gets his corrections immediately within the medium of approach; namely, by hearing his "model" reading correctly and fluently. If the student reads "was," and the tutor reads "saw," the message is immediately apparent. Accordingly, the student will try to pronounce the word in the same way his tutor did next time he has a chance. It may take several occasions to accomplish this aim.

This approach is effective because it keeps the student from becoming frustrated and discouraged by being constantly told that he is wrong. Older poor readers almost anticipate this "fussing" or "nagging" as they perceive interruptions and corrections. Negative reactions are kept to a minimum and further trials at reading are thus encouraged. The teacher/tutor remains the silent mentor, but readily answers questions raised by the student. Comments by the teacher are positively stated; remarks like "I told you that before," have no place here.

Reading material used for the impress sessions is also unique in the sense that it does not have to be specially prepared or programmed. Reading materials are taken from existing textbooks selected for a given grade level. Newspaper articles, magazines, catalogs, and books, can also be used and often meet the student's motivational needs better than tritely written school texts. The method focuses on fluency or flow of reading; accuracy is obtained from modeling behavior. Instead of lengthy sessions or formal classes, frequent short periods of reading together are recommended. Moreover, adjunct school personnel and lay volunteers can be used with great success.

The theoretical basis on which the impress method is built is the idea that reading is a neurological and brain process. Somehow the brain has not been sufficiently impressed or imprinted in older poor readers and deserves another try.

Modified Alphabet and Spelling Forms

Techniques and approaches which attempt to make English spelling regular in one way or another fall into this category. The idea behind these special methods is that English spelling does not represent a direct correspondence between sound and symbol, and this lack of a one-to-one relationship between sound and symbol makes reading more difficult.

Among the many methods which have taken this remedial avenue is the i.t.a., or Initial Teaching Alphabet, developed in Great Britain and the United States to simplify reading by adding more characters to the existing alphabet. The student does not have to learn several pronunciations for one and the same letter, such as voiced and voiceless (unvoiced) "TH" in the words "the" and "teeth." "A gaeme ov baull" in i.t.a. is our conventional "a game of ball." The difficulty comes when the switch from i.t.a. to conventional English spelling must be initiated because newspaper articles and books are not written in i.t.a. symbols.

There are several other methods which attempt to regularize English spelling, most of them taking the phonetic approach to accomplish this. For example, color clues can be given which indicate to the reader what sound is needed for what symbol by giving certain colors to certain symbols (letters or letter combinations), which, in turn, tell the reader how these color clues are sounded or what they stand for. One of the more widely used methods of color clues is Gattegno's Words-in-Color Method, which was first used in England. In most instances, these methods are more helpful with beginners in reading than with older poor readers, but several claim success with older students and adults.

Two drawbacks to such methods are that they provide (1) an artificial "crutch" that must be removed at some point and (2) they require specially prepared materials. However, a new method usually is accompanied by high motivation for the reader as well as the teacher. Sometimes a fresh approach is greatly needed, and, in that case, such methods may be helpful.

Programmed Approaches

Programmed approaches to remediation have grown out of attempts by behavioral psychologists to break down a given task into small units, or "frames," and present them to the learner one at a time, step by step, until he masters the frame. Each completed step in a programmed series is reinforcing because of the intrinsic feeling of mastery. One of the more widely used approaches in this category is the Sullivan Reading Program, which is available commercially in seriated booklets.

In the programmed, or cloze technique, the student is given a sentence in which a letter, word, or phrase is left out (blank). The student is required to write in the missing word based on information fed to him in previous steps in the program. Immediate feedback of correct answers is given in a column which lists the answers, usually in the left margin of the same page. The method appeals to older students because of its step-by-step progression and immediate feedback of correct answers. Incorrect responses are kept to a minimum and the student is allowed to progress at his own speed without embarrassment. Here is a sample:

Correct Responses   *Sample Sentence* (based on previously
POLICEMAN   read material)
TICKET   The _____ gave my father a _____
CAR   because he had parked his _____ on the
                          sidewalk.

The Structural Linguistics Approach

The structural linguistics approach to the teaching of reading is based in part on two fairly recent developments. Gestalt psychology and modern linguistics have combined to give us "psycholinguistics" as a new approach. Both disciplines examine the configuration and structure of a design or object. In terms of language, it is the structure of the language which is the basis for a didactic technique. The sentence can be considered the basic element of thought in its written form. Words, likewise, can be broken down into basic elements, like affixes and suffixes, and ultimately letters or letter combinations. From a phonetic standpoint, the basic structure is the sound unit (phoneme). Once the sentence or word is broken down into its structural subcomponents, it can again be built up synthetically to take on configuration and total structure, like building blocks can be used to build a structure.

For example, the small structural unit *at* can be combined with initial consonants to form words:

c/at   f/at   r/at   s/at   h/at   b/at   m/at   p/at   v/at

This building game can be applied to larger structures and substructures as well, either in whole words or sentences. For instance, the suffix -ing can be combined with basic root words to form new variations and combinations of the basic word stem plus its ending: standing, walking, talking, etc. The student is asked to observe and recognize the structural elements, use them as building blocks, or recognize them in embedded forms, such as -at (cat), -ing (working), or un- (undesirable). New words become at least partially familiar to the reader because of the recognition and recall of familiar parts previously encountered in other situations.

One advantage of the recognition or "sight" method lies in its systematic presentation of structural familiarity with words and sentences. Structure can be found in sound (phonetic elements) as well as in written form (visual elements), making the method workable in a combined audiovisual approach to reading. Another advantage of this approach is that the reader's perceptual powers are being sharpened by phonetic and visual recognition of structures. Specific exercises designed to develop perceptual powers are found in Chapters 4 and 5.

The Structural Linguistics Approach can also be used with older poor readers in order to help them attack longer and more complex words. It allows for elementary as well as more advanced vocabulary needed by older students.

The Phonetic Approach

The sound approach has already been discussed in detail in Chapter 4 and needs no further mention here except for inclusion of the category for the sake of completeness.

SELECTING THE MOST EFFECTIVE METHOD OR TECHNIQUE

No one methodological approach is superior to another for all students and all teachers. One person may use a method with great enthusiasm and achieve good results, while another teacher might reluctantly adopt a method because she was told to do so and consequently has little proof of success. In most cases, it is advisable to combine methods to the best advantage of the learner. For example, a structural linguistics approach can effectively be combined with the use of color cues, one reinforcing and enhancing the other.

With older poor readers, care must be exercised in the selection of the methodological approach because many techniques are designed primarily for beginning readers at a much younger age. "See the cat run!" can delight a first grader but bore a 16-year-old adolescent. On the other hand, "Fix the carburetor, Mac!" might be just the right sentence for our teenager. A list of publishers who specialize in high-interest, low-readability materials is presented in Appendix C.

Of course, selection of a suitable remedial approach also depends on the student's strength and deficiencies. For example, one would hardly choose a purely phonetic approach with a hard-of-hearing person or a student whose main strength is phonics but still cannot read well. The remainder of this chapter presents a variety of practical, tested exercises which can be employed with older poor readers especially. These exercises are not presented in any specific sequence, nor are they representative of certain methods and techniques. Instead, the exercises are developed around specific skills. In order to facilitate selection of the exercises and to show something of their purpose, the following coding system has been developed:

Code	Skill Category
VP	Visual Perception
VM	Visual Memory
AP	Auditory Perception
AM	Auditory Memory
T-K	Tactile-Kinesthetic
OS	Orientation in Space
L-R	Left-Right Discrimination or L-R Directionality
F-G	Figure-Ground Relationship

Applicability of a given exercise is closely related to the assessment described in Chapter 2. The code appears at the beginning of each individual exercise in this chapter. A quick overview of available categories can be obtained by referring to the "Quick Educational Prescription Finder" at the end of this chapter (p. 146). This prescription finder lists each exercise in Chapters 4 and 5 along with its corresponding codes. Most exercises fall into more than one skill category.

EXERCISES FOR DEVELOPING SPECIFIC SKILLS

Exercise 5.1 *Sandtray Writing*

Skill Code: T-K, also VP, AP, and L-R.

Objective: Reinforcement of perception and execution of letters and words by using a tactile-kinesthetic approach. Strengthening of left-right directionality to avoid reversals. Visual-phonetic impressions to accompany tactile-kinesthetic experiences.

Materials: Cookie tray filled with sand, rice, grits, or other abrasive material (Photo 5-1). For more advanced students, a cement floor, rug, or sandpaper are suitable surfaces.

Instructions: Use this exercise especially with students who have difficulty with reversals: b for d, or was for saw, etc. Ask the student to write letters and words on the tray using the index finger of his preferred hand. Ask him to say the letter or word as he writes it in the sand. Refer to p. 62 in Chapter 2 for a list of letters and words that are frequently reversed. After simpler words are mastered, introduce more complex words, like plot and pilot, fled and felt, etc.

Photo 5-1

Photo 5-2

Assist the student's transfer of his newly acquired skills by having him use a stick to write in the sand somewhere on the playground (Photo 5-2), and later, by writing the same words on a sheet of paper. Frequency of errors will guide the teacher in determining the need for further exercises with the sand tray.

Exercise 5.2   *Writing-in-Air*

Skill Code: T-K, also L-R and VM.

Objective: Reinforcement of visual memory through T-K sensory avenues. L-R also considered as training in directionality on the written page (space).

Materials: None.

Instructions: The exercise is designed for students who have graduated from the basic tasks in Exercise 5.1. Ask the student to write words in the air using the index finger of his preferred hand. At first, simple words should be used, but, for the advanced learner, longer and more complex words can be introduced since the air space has no limits. A game activity can be added by asking one student to write the "mystery word" in the air while by-standers have to guess it. The student who does the "air writing" has to stand in front of the group with his back turned.

Exercise 5.3   *Bare-Back Writing*

Skill Code: T-K.

Objective: Same as 5.1 and 5.2.

Material: None.

Instructions: For further reinforcement of letter and word writing, skin impressions can be used successfully with hardcore poor readers. Ask one student to write simple words and letters on the back of a partner (Photo 5-3). You may show a few examples first, then ask the students to do the same. Other cutaneous surfaces, such as the palm of the hand or the arms, can be used also.

Exercise 5.4   *Homemade Jigsaw Puzzles*

Skill Code: OS and VP, some T-K.

Objective: Strengthening of visual perceptions and orientation in space (rotations).

Materials: Sheets of construction paper, scissors, pencil, and ruler.

Instructions: A simple and inexpensive way to make jigsaw puzzles is outlined below Homemade puzzles are superior to commercially produced puzzles because they are inexpensively produced

Photo 5-3

and their difficulty level can be adjusted as needed. Primary considerations in making these puzzles must be shape and the relationship of parts to one another.

Note: No pictorial ornamentations should be placed on the puzzles as these distract from the primary purpose of training, which is visual perception and orientation in space.

Take a sheet of construction paper or similar material and draw lines on it to make simple designs. Cut along the penciled lines with scissors to obtain the pieces for the puzzle. Mix the pieces and ask the student to put them together. You may wish to keep a design sheet prior to cutting up the construction paper when more complex designs are attempted.

If the student has great difficulty with making the design, help him by letting him feel the outer edges of the pieces. Let him put two and three pieces together first. If he fails, show him how, and then ask him again to do the puzzle. Use some color coding for pieces in close proximity to aid in completion of the puzzle. Use "oral language" when explaining things: "This rounded piece goes here where you can also see and feel a rounded piece!"

Figure 5-1 shows several designs ranging from simple to complex models.

Figure 5-1

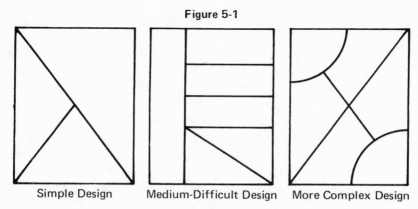

Simple Design   Medium-Difficult Design   More Complex Design

Exercise 5.5   *Paper Grids and Boards*

Skill Code: OS, T-K and VP.

Objective: Strengthening spatial orientation by developing ability to copy simple designs in the environment, with the ultimate purpose being to recognize shapes of letters and words and to reproduce them accurately on a page. The rationale here is that pegboard exercises strengthen visual perception, a contributing aspect of reading. Both developmental and complexity levels have to be taken into account during these exercises. Students with gross motor difficulties and coordination problems, usually the very low level readers, may have to be started on a wooden board with pegs. More advanced students can begin by using paper and pencil.

Materials: Pegboard (wooden or fiberboard), pegs (golf-tees), paper and pencil, or crayons.

Instructions: First, show the student a design on the board (wooden or paper) and ask him to copy it. The designs should become more complex and intricate as the student progresses in proficiency. After the use of pegs or pencils, colors may be introduced for even sharper observations. Designs should move from large to small, simple to complex, and from an up-down emphasis to a left-right one. At an even later stage, letters can replace abstract designs, like copying an A or F.

Second, greater difficulty can also be introduced by establishing the design farther away from the student's position so that the perceptual task of observing the model becomes even more difficult. A design may be displayed at the blackboard, with students in their seats being asked to copy it on their paper formboards.

A sample for wooden board designs, featuring an abstract design and the letter F, is shown in Figure 5-2A. Figure 5-2B through E are samples of paper formboard designs, with a copy exercise drawn into each. The student can be asked to copy the designs on a separate sheet, or in cases of difficulty, he may simply continue the design on the same sheet, moving from left to right on the formboard page.

Figure 5-2A

Two Sample Designs for the Wooden Pegboard

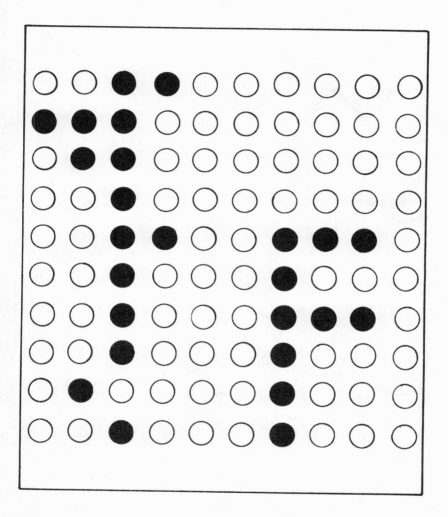

Figure 5-2B

Paper Formboard, Simple Designs

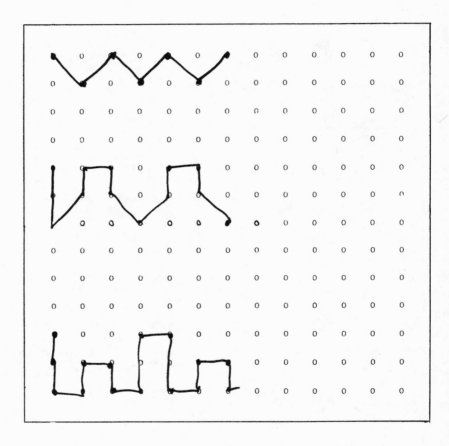

Figure 5-2C

Paper Formboard, More Complex Designs

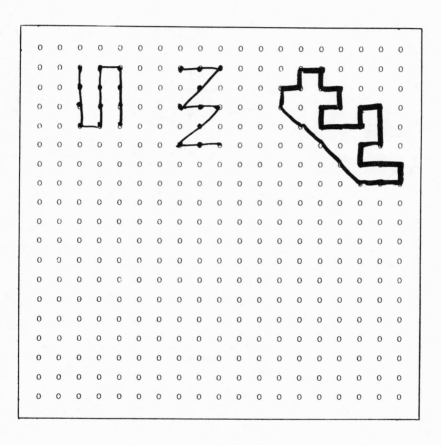

Figure 5-2D

Paper Formboard, More Spaced Layout

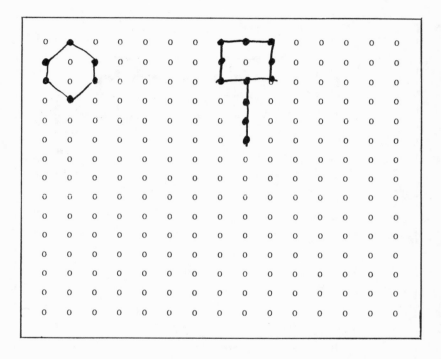

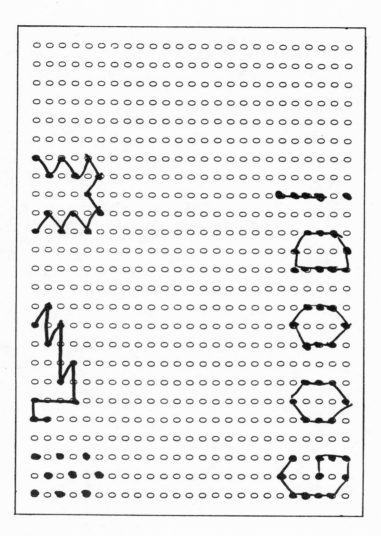

Figure 5-2E

Paper Formboard, Less Spaced Layout

Exercise 5.6   *L-R Eye Movements in Space*
                                                Eye-Hand Coordination

Skill Code: OS, L-R.

Objective: Establishing firmly the left-right orientation on a page by using color coding for reinforcement. Developing hand-eye coordination for purposes of establishing directionality.

Materials: Paper, newspaper, red and green crayons.

Instructions: Ask the students to prepare sheets of lined paper by drawing a vertical line in the *left* margin using a *green* color, and another vertical line in the *right* margin using a *red* color. These lines will help to condition the student's movements on the page. *Green* stands for *go!* and *red* for *stop!* allowing a transfer from familiar traffic signals. Ask students to use the sheets thus prepared for all their written exercises.

In cases where difficulties are pronounced—i.e., where left-right directionality is poorly established—ask students to bring old newspapers, prepare the large pages in the same manner as above, and let them make sweeping movements from green to red, or left to right, on the papers, thereby coordinating hand and eye actions. At first, crayons may be used, then pencil, and ultimately words can replace simple lines and wavy patterns across the page. Here is an example to illustrate the exercise:

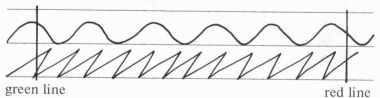

green line   red line

Exercise 5.7   *Figure-Ground Color Coding*

Skill Code: F-G (Visual).

Objective: Lifting words from the visual-perceptual background into the student's foreground making the written word stand out and bring out structural aspects of the written text.

Materials: Colored pencils or crayons, prepared or ordinary text.

Instructions: Ask the student to underline certain parts of words, or certain words in complete sentences, using colored crayons or pencils so that they stand out for easy recognition. Prepared or ordinary texts can be used for this purpose. For instance, ask the student to *underline in red* the letter combination (morphograph) *AR* in a prepared exercise like this:

car   bark   tar   farther   market   lark   cart   target

Students who have difficulty recognizing the definite and indefinite articles (the and a) can be asked to underline them, using different colors for each, like red for *the,* and blue for *a.* Mixing up these two articles is a common error in poor readers.

Some poor readers have difficulty recognizing vowels and double vowels (diphthongs). Here again the exercise can prove helpful to the student. Ask the student to underline or circle vowel combinations like these:

bear   fear   pea   treat   appeal   reap   leaper   feast

This is an exercise in visual perception since the pronunciation of the vowel combination "ea" may vary. To avoid confusion at first,

words can be grouped according to like pronunciation: bear, tear, or read, bead, repeat,
etc.

Exercise 5.8   *Use of Tape Recorder*

Skill Code: AP, with VP combined.

Objective: Combining auditory and visual perception to
work in unison, with nonverbal corrections as
feedback.

Materials: Tape recorder or cassette recorder, blank tape or
cassette, textbook, reading material or prepared
exercise.

Instructions: Ask the student to read a passage into the
microphone. You may read the passage first
together if he has difficulty with the passage.
Next, let the student listen to his recording
with you. Whenever a mistake occurs, you
and/or the student must raise a hand or tap
on the table with your fingers signaling that a
mistake has been recognized. The student
follows the written text as he listens to the
recording. Now, both of you listen once
more and write down errors for subsequent
discussion and further drill. In this way the
student has a chance to learn about and
correct errors peculiar to his own reading
habits, rather than get involved in exercises
he may not need.

Exercise 5.9   *Reading and the Typewriter*

Skill Code: T-K, in connection with AP and VP.

Objective: Employing tactile-kinesthetic sensory modalities
to facilitate writing skills and reinforce word
recognition by tactile reinforcement.

Materials: Manual typewriter and paper.

Instructions: These exercises are recommended especially for students with handwriting difficulty (dysgraphia) that slows down their learning. A hunt-and-peck method may be used, or, for a more thorough training experience, the touch system can be introduced. This method can be further enhanced by color-coding fingernails and keys on the typewriter. Prepared programs are now commercially available.

Ask the student to transcribe some of his written exercises using the typewriter. He may type single words or whole sentences. In the beginning, words with certain stem or prefix characteristics should be used for repetitive drill.

Examples: cat, fat, hat, sat, rat, pat, mat, etc.
fin, win, tin, shin, din, etc.
steal, peal, team, lean, ream, etc.

Exercise 5.10   *Auditory Foreground*

Skill Code: F-G (aural) and AP.

Objective: Aiding in auditory perception by differentiating between foreground and background in sound production of spoken words or sentences.

Materials: None, or tape recorder.

Instructions: Ask the student to listen very carefully as you or a helper say words and, later, sentences. Tell him to watch out for certain sounds or sound combinations contained in the spoken words or sentences. Ask him to tell you what letters or words he heard. For instance, ask him what words contained the AR combinations in this sentence:

I saw cars passing by the barn.
(Answer: cars and barn)

If the student shows difficulty in recognizing the word segments auditorily, raise your voice slightly to emphasize them when you come to the parts.

Exercise 5.11   *What's Missing?*

Skill Code: VM.

Objective: Training visual memory skills by employing visual imagery.

Materials: Small objects of any kind (pins, paper clips, pencils, erasers, etc.).

Instructions: Place several small objects on the table and invite the student to study the display for one minute. Then, ask him to look aside (or walk away for a moment) while you take one object away. Ask the student to guess which one was taken, then repeat the game. Another version is to switch one object; i.e., move it in a different place, and ask the student which object is in a new location. The exercise can be played by the students themselves and needs little supervison. Instead of removing an object, a new one may be added to the display.

Exercise 5.12   *What Did You See?*

Skill Code: VM, also T-K.

Objective: Developing visual memory by reproducing designs or words when the stimulus object is removed.

Materials: Blackboard or sheet of paper, chalk or pencil.

Instructions: Write a word on the board or draw a design of any kind. After exposing the design for a minute or less, ask the student to draw it from memory. Vary exposure time and complexity of designs or words.

Exercise 5.13

Tangrams

Skill Code: VP, OS.

Objective: Arranging designs made from smaller pieces (parts) to strengthen visual perception of a total (Configuration or Gestalt).

Materials: Small, flat shapes cut out of wood, cardboard, or paper.

Instructions: Obtain small wooden pieces as contained in puzzles and games for children, or ask students to cut out shapes (squares, triangles, etc.) from cardboard. Ask students either to copy designs previously prepared, or let them create their own designs. Verbalize corrections of student errors in copy work by explaining to them why the errors were made; e.g., lack of observation of relationships, etc. See Figure 5-3 for illustration of tangrams.

Figure 5-3

**Arranging Tangrams Helps Visual Perception
and Orientation in Space**

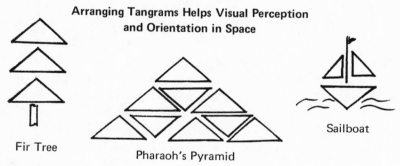

Fir Tree

Pharaoh's Pyramid

Sailboat

Tangrams can be traced with templates or laid out
with wooden chips or cardboard cutouts.

Exercise 5.14   *Explorations into Outer Space*

Skill Code: OS, L-R.

Objective: Following instructions using various directions on a page, with emphasis on left-right movements and orientation.

Materials: Cardboard, ruler, felt-tipped pen, buttons (several colors or shapes) to use as markers.

Instructions: This game-type exercise consists of a board with squares drawn on it, as shown in Figure 5-4A. A number of chips are made from small cardboard squares on which the directions are written as instructions, as shown in Figure 5-4B. Before the game is attempted, students should be given rules orally and by demonstration on the gameboard. The game is suitable for use with two to four players.

Rules require that each student, in turn, takes a chip from a previously shuffled pile of chips and executes the command given on the chip. When the instructions call for a move *right* or a move *up left,* the student places his button in the center square to start, and then moves his button one square in the given direction. A tutor or mentor is present to supervise the correctness of placement. The buttons are always placed in relation to the previously obtained position. The game is ended and the winner is declared when one player reaches the outer edge of the board (OUTER SPACE) first. The game is continued until all players have reached OUTER SPACE. If errors in directional moves occur, the tutor/mentor makes the necessary corrections. No punishment is given for the error other than losing a turn for the player who made the error. A suffi-

Figure 5-4A

Explorations into Outer Space Game

Gameboard

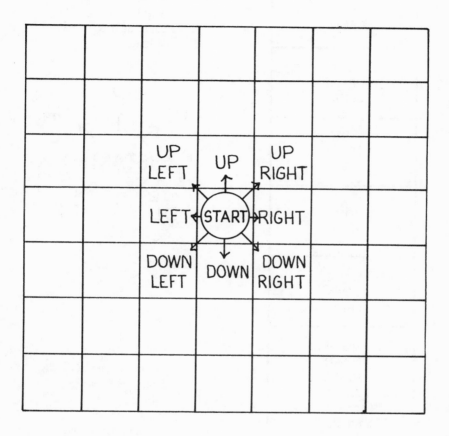

Figure 5-4B

MOVE LEFT
MOVE UP LEFT
MOVE UP RIGHT
MOVE RIGHT
MOVE DOWN LEFT
MOVE DOWN RIGHT
MOVE UP
MOVE DOWN

Below: The eight possibilities of directional movements on the gameboard. A spin bottle could be used instead of chips.

Duplicate and cut apart the list at the left. You will then have eight paper chips to use in playing the "Explorations into Outer Space" game for reinforcement of left-right discrimination. Two sets of chips will suffice for two players.

cient number of chips is needed to play the game, at least two of each of the eight different instructions (directions) as shown in Figure 5-4B. The various possible moves by one player in a given game are shown in Figure 5-4C. It is possible that two or more players may have their chips in the same square at a given time.

Instead of Left-Right, directions on a map may be substituted (N, NW, W, SW, S, etc.)

Figure 5-4C

Winning Moves from START to OUTER SPACE

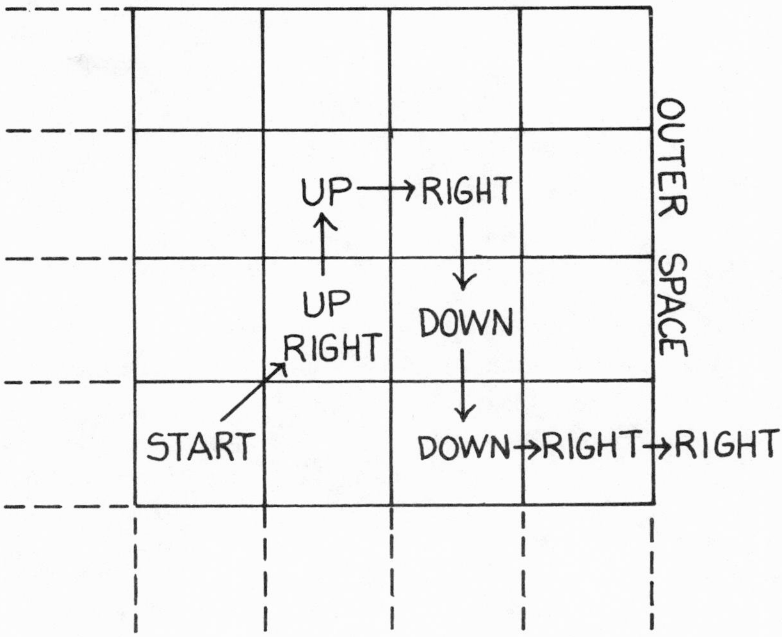

The Gameboard (Figure 5-4A) can be mimeographed so that Players can actually trace their moves on the paperboard.

Exercise 5.15   *Word Domino*

Skill Code: VP.

Objective: Quick word recognition by visual discrimination of like and different words and sentences.

Materials: Small index cards or cardboard pieces.

Instructions: Prepare a set of small cards. Divide each in half by drawing a line down the middle of the card. Write words in each half. Players receive an equal number of cards. The game is played in a fashion similar to dominoes by adding on to the ends of a card series, as shown below. The player who has used up his cards first is the winner.

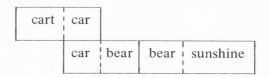

Exercise 5.16   *Is There Such a Word?*

Skill Code: VP and AP.

Objective: Building words through structural elements.

Materials: Cardboard cards.

Instructions: This game-type exercise is played like "Authors." Several sets of cards are prepared, with four cards to the set. In the beginning, 10 to 15 sets will suffice to play the game. At the top right of each card, the basic structural word is written. Four words using that basic structure are written in the middle of the card, as follows:

BROWN   OPERATE   BATH

browned   operator   bather

browns	operating	bathing
browning	operation	bathed
brownish	operated	bathes

Players now try to get as many complete sets as possible by asking their partners, in turn, if they have a given card, say "operation." If they do not get the card from the addressed player, they may take a new card from the deck in the middle of the table. The player with the highest number of complete sets is the winner.

Exercise 5.17   *Scrambled Sentences*

Skill Code: VP, OS, L-R.

Objective: Developing a feeling for structural arrangement using word recognition skills, sequential order of sentences, and L-R directionality.

Materials: Paper and pencil, or prepared mimeographed exercise sheets.

Instructions: Prepare sheets with scrambled sentences on them, one sentence per line. Leave the next line blank for students' rearrangement of words for meaning. There might be more than one correct solution for a given sentence. Examples of scrambled sentences:

car see the !

went baseball yesterday I game a to.
car not did my start.

see the did cop at you corner the?

Exercise 5.18   *Pick-a-Card*

Skill Code: VP.

Objective: Quick word recognition, competitive drill.

Materials: Small index cards, felt-tipped pen.

Instructions: Print single words or short phrases on small index cards. Place cards face down on a table. Two or more students take turns in picking up a card and trying to read it. If they can read the word or phrase, they may keep the card. If they cannot read it, the card is returned to the pile and the pile is shuffled. When all cards have been picked, each participant counts his cards. The student with the highest number of cards is the winner and may get a prize. The teacher/tutor goes over the rest of the cards helping the participants with word analysis and recognition. Then the game is played again. Care must be exercised so that selected students have similar reading levels in order to keep the competitive factor to a minimum but still provide a challenge to the participants.

Exercise 5.19   *Finding Your Way*

Skill Code: OS.

Objective: Helping to develop orientation in space, following directions, and reading names on maps.

Materials: City maps, state maps, small index cards.

Instructions: Ask the student to come along on a walk or field trip using the map. Study the map first by pointing out major cities and landmarks as they appear written on the map. Then ask students to make up their own routes or trips by copying names and landmarks on small cards. Cards are then arranged to follow the sequence of names which make up the trip. As one student calls out the names (New York! Niagara Falls! Washington, D.C.! Byrd Park!), another one follows the route on the map with his finger, calling out the names when he has found their location.

*   *   *   *   *   *   *   *

A QUICK EDUCATIONAL PRESCRIPTION FINDER

Chapters 4 and 5 describe a variety of exercises that can be successfully incorporated in remedial approaches. The exercises were presented in numerical order and under categorical sub-headings. In order to provide still another way of classifying the exercises, a *Quick Educational Prescription Finder* has been prepared as a ready reference and index to the various exercises.

The Prescription Finder which follows lists all exercises in Chapters 4 and 5 in the left column and shows an "x" in the appropriate columns marked "Area of Remediation" at the top of the Finder. Thus, if a teacher or tutor wishes to single out exercises specifically in the area of Auditory Perception, she does not have to leaf through two entire chapters to find the appropriate exercises but can find *all* exercises primarily related to auditory perception by going down the respective column marked AP and then locating the exercises by number in the left column.

Another advantage of the Prescription Finder is that it represents a starting point for the teacher's own collection of and addition to exercises contained in the book. Newly located exercises from outside sources can be recorded on index cards, with the same subheadings as in this book, and then entered in the Finder where some lines have been left blank for future use. The Prescription Finder thus provides a system or aid for classifying newly acquired material for ready reference.

Quick Educational Prescription Finder

Explanation of Symbols:

Code	Category	Code	Category
VP	Visual Perception	T-K	Tactile-Kinesthetic
VM	Visual Memory	OS	Orientation in Space
AP	Auditory Perception	L-R	Left-Right Discrimination or L-R Directionality
AM	Auditory Memory	F-G	Figure-Ground Relationship

Number of Exercise	Game	Area of Remediation								✓
		VP	VM	AP	AM	T-K	OS	L-R	F-G	
4.1				X	X					
4.2				X	X					
4.3				X						
4.4				X						
4.5				X						
4.6				X						
4.7		X		X						
4.8		X		X						
4.9				X	X					
4.10	X	X						X		
4.11										
4.12		X								
4.13		X								
4.14		X								
4.15		X								
5.1						X		X	X	
5.2						X	X	X		
5.3						X		X		
5.4		X				X	X			
5.5		X				X		X		

Number of Exercise	Game	Area of Remediation								√
		VP	VM	AP	AM	T-K	OS	L-R	F-G	
5.6							X	X		
5.7									X	
5.8	X	X		X						
5.9						X				
5.10				X					X	
5.11			X							
5.12			X			X				
5.13		X					X			
5.14	X						X	X		
5.15	X	X								
5.16	X	X		X						
5.17		X					X	X		
5.18	X	X								
5.19	X						X			

Chapter Summary

This chapter presents an organized framework for the most commonly used remedial methods and techniques. The Multi-Sensory Approach attempts to bring in many sensory avenues which lead to successful reading, rather than relying on auditory and visual senses alone. The Impress Method stands out because of its apparent simplicity and because it minimizes criticism leveled against the poor reader. The Programmed Approach is based on B.F. Skinner's important work in the area of behavioral modification and has as its advantage the breaking down of big tasks into small segments or frames, and the offering of built-in reinforcement.

Many remedial methods have attempted to help the poor reader by making English orthography more regular, thus more simple and easier to grasp. Among the various methods using this approach are techniques employing color coding for the various sounds of the letters or introducing new symbols to make the sound-symbol relationship more regular and logical. The Structural Linguistics Approach was born out of new insights gained from teaching English grammar and from work by psychologists and linguists concerned with the Gestalt or configuration of objects around us.

In addition to describing the basic approaches to reading (with no claim to completeness), the chapter provides the teacher with specific exercises to help older poor readers in areas of most frequent difficulty. At times, deficits exist at much deeper layers than those tapped by conventional reading techniques, such as perceptual training, left-right orientation, or a sense of directionality. Training and retraining these deeper layers of the learning strata will strengthen the poor reader's basic skills and help prepare him for more successful reading as well as for enjoyment of reading activities.

Teachers will find the Quick Educational Prescription Finder at the end of the chapter helpful as a quick index to specific categories of remediation. The Prescription Finder can also be used as a basic classification system for additional exercises the teacher may encounter during her work.

6

Comprehending
What Is Being Read

In a general sense, the skill of reading includes both word recognition and comprehension. If we were asked to read a passage in a language which was unknown to us, at best we would be able to sound out the passage, but we would be unable to understand what we read. Thus, the reading process is not complete unless we understand what we read.

Some people can read with fair accuracy and speed but do not comprehend what they have just read. If this is the case, then the specific problem is not one of recognizing the printed letters and words on the page and sounding out their phonetic equivalents, but of comprehending the meaning of the words and sentences. Small children who have excellent phonetic abilities sometimes sound out words above their level of comprehension and fail to get the meaning of the word because their comprehension skill or cognitive level is below their word recognition ability.

Thus word recognition skills and comprehension are integral parts of the reading process and should be taught together.

However, if one of them is weaker than the other, appropriate exercises must be found to remediate the condition. The so-called "word callers" can be helped through intensive training in comprehension and memory skills.

MEANING RELATED TO READING

As an example, let us assume that the reader has read the familiar saying, "A stitch in time saves nine." Even though he may have been able to read the sentence—that is, to say the words—he may still not know what the sentence means. Mere ability to master word recognition skills will not be sufficient. Our reader might have the literal comprehension to state that the sentence has something to do with sewing and stitches, while someone else might come up with the statement, "If you do something right away you can avoid trouble later on!" Still another person might say that all of this is encompassed by the concept "prevention."

We must be concerned with both literal and interpretive comprehension, both being levels of the cognitive process. The more we function toward the abstract pole of the concrete-abstract continuum, the better we can make use of our reading. As an example, the word table can be a concrete matter of assembled pieces of wood or steel, or it may be considered a utilitarian device for serving food, or it may be viewed as a part of the overall concept "furniture." The diagram in Figure 6-1 explains the various levels of abstraction in a hierarchic order of succession which moves from the concrete (literal) meaning to the levels where conceptual thinking needs to be applied to the fullest benefit of the reader.

People with difficulties in the area of logical, abstract, and inferential thinking can be helped by exercises in which the tutor focuses directly on logic and abstract thinking. Both tutor and student think out loud, together. The diagram in Figure 6-1 can aid in this teaching process by actually showing the way a concrete thought is elevated to higher abstract levels. The word abstract comes from the Latin verb *abstrahere*, meaning to pull away from. We are pulling away from the concrete verbatim meaning of the words and sentences to higher levels of meaning. It is like climbing a ladder, rung by rung, higher and higher. The higher we climb, the better we can see the surrounding territory in its context.

Figure 6-1

The Concrete-Abstract Dimension of Thinking

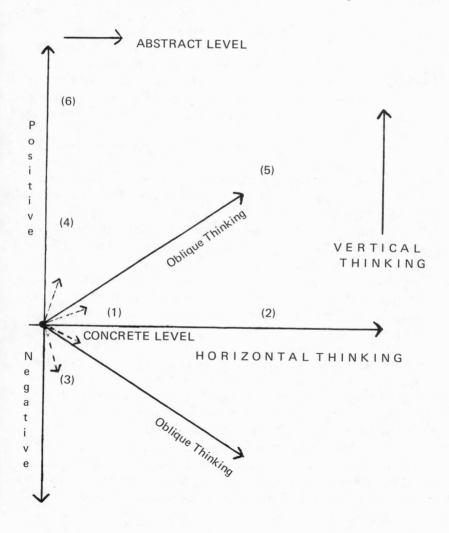

Let's have another look at the diagram and follow one example through the various stages and positions on the concrete-abstract hierarchical dimension. The statements which follow are numbered according to corresponding levels of thinking presented in Figure 6-1. The encircled numbers in the diagram will facilitate locating the positions of the statements along the hierarchy.

1. *An apple a day keeps the doctor away.* This is the original version of the familiar saying, stated positively and concretely. The meaning expressed in the saying is taken from everyday experiences of people in bygone days when proverbs and sayings were used to warn or instill moral values. "A vitamin pill a day keeps the doctor away" would express a similar warning or encouragement. It is stated on the same level of concreteness.

2. *A stitch in time saves nine.* This statement expresses the same idea as was said in No. 1, above, only with different words. It is a lateral or horizontal translation in the diagram. There is little abstract thinking in this translation. It is just a rehash of the same statement using different words and images.

3. *An apple a day does not keep the doctor away.* This is Statement No. 1, above, expressed negatively. It does not bring us any new information but may help us think in a different way, looking at the statement from still another concrete angle. Its argumentative, negative nature might help some people in returning to the positive plane, but this time with more abstract meaning.

4. *Taking something early might help us later.* In this statement, we not only have changed the original words but we also have pulled away (abstracted) from the original and concrete version. We are no longer concerned with an apple, and the doctor is not the only one we want to keep away. This is semi-abstract thinking, in the positive direction.

5. *Maybe apples help us, but why not try bananas?* This statement also takes us away from the concrete meaning, but not in the right (upward) direction. We are straying away from the upward path and may even make irrelevant contributions. This can lead to fallacious thinking, not implied in the original

statement. It can be misleading and bring poor or false answers. Paranoid and schizophrenic people sometimes think on bizarre and oblique levels.

6. *We can prevent some problems.* Our last example, finally, expresses the highest level of abstraction for the original statement. Note that we no longer talk about such concrete things as apples and doctors because they were just given as examples anyway. It is immaterial whether we are mentioning the doctor, butcher, baker, or candlestick maker. The central and main idea, as the highest form of abstraction, is *prevention.*

Comprehending and thinking cannot be taught overnight. It is a long process, but one that will eventually lead to positive results. The more we can get out of our reading, the more efficient our reading will be. Abstracting, thinking, and intelligence are related. A retarded child thinks on the more concrete level, while a gifted one thinks in abstract terms (or, he has the potential to do so). The point is that thinking, like reading or other skills, can be remediated and improvements can be obtained by employing appropriate techniques and methods. Some suggestions for exercises in abstract thinking follow.

SUGGESTIONS FOR REMEDIAL EXERCISES

The level of remediation depends on the age of the child, the degree of his ability and intellectual development, in addition to whatever handicap he might present.

Classification Exercises

The ability to classify objects in our environment is the basis for perception and conceptualization. Classification serves to reduce the chaos, and helps us to make sense out of nonsense. According to Piaget, the Swiss psychologist, classifying objects is one of the first tasks the child must learn.

Exercise 6.1   *The Sorting Box*

The student is provided with a box containing a large number of various objects, like pins, nails, film, slips of paper, colored cards, buttons, paper clips, etc. The selection must spread over a wide variety of things with different colors, shapes, sizes, and materials. The assortment is placed in a *Sorting Box.*

Photo 6-1

**The Sorting Box Helps to Categorize
Objects as a First Step in Developing Comprehension**

The student is asked to sort the objects in the box by laying them out on the table. He may be asked first to arrange the objects in two piles, like metal versus nonmetal objects, chromatic versus achromatic (black and white) colors, large versus small, etc. Later, when the student has demonstrated proficiency in sorting, he may be asked to sort the objects in three or more piles, always observing and verbally expressing the reasons behind his sorting by naming the common attributes of each pile. Errors are discussed with the teacher or tutor, and necessary corrections follow. A sorting arrangement is shown in Photo 6-1.

Like/Not Alike Exercises

Objects of various shapes and designs are placed in front of the student and he is asked to show which ones are alike and which ones are not alike. A student with a greater degree of deficiency may first manipulate actual objects: squares, triangles, and diamonds in three dimensions. Later, he is transferred to written exercises drawn on a sheet of paper. The following examples may serve as guides to levels of difficulty.

Exercise 6.2   *Which One Is Different?*
Which One Does Not Belong There?

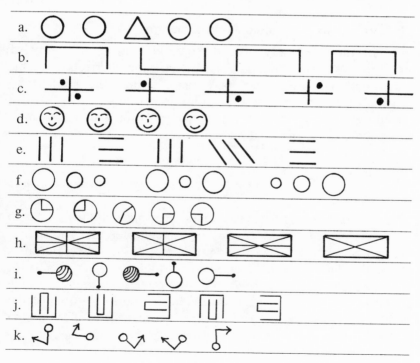

o.	55	45	35	12	85	15
p.	3	4	12	6	8	24	10
q.	shoe	glove	sock	hand	nose
r.	gas	rain	car	sky	growth
s.	spoon	shovel	knife	fork	ladle
t.	hot	cool	warm	cold	temperature

Symbolization by Gradual Approximation

In the same way as a person must make order out of meaningless surroundings by classifying objects in his environment, so another task may require the student to recognize an object whose meaning is not yet clear. Clues are given to the observer in form, shape, or color which allow him to conceptualize the final meaning.

Exercise 6.3   *What Is It?*
What Might It Be?

Color slides of various themes and topics are inserted into the slide projector and shown on a screen, but first the slide is shown out of focus (by turning the lens until the slide picture is blurred). The students are asked to identify what the image they see on the screen *might* be. If no one can guess it, the slide is brought into sharper focus, gradually, until the topic of the slide picture is named correctly; e.g., a street scene, a car, a man leaning against a tree, etc.

Exercise 6.4   *What Word Will It Be?*

The procedure is the same as under Exercise 6.3, except that slides with *words* are used instead of concrete pictures. Again the slide is first shown out of focus and students are asked to try to identify the word. This is not "word guessing" in the narrower sense since the viewers will eventually be shown the correct word in focus, thus obtaining realistic feedback. But the contours and Gestalt of the image will allow them to observe clues very carefully. The teacher may point out that a given word flashed on the screen, while still appearing blurred, might have a tall letter at the beginning, and a letter which extends downward at the end (e.g., as in the word *telling*). The "middle hump" where two "l's" are, also may serve as a landmark for word recognition. When the image comes into sharper focus, the student might recognize the familiar suffix -ing.

Hierarchical Abstraction and Drawing Inferences

As was pointed out earlier in this chapter, some students have difficulty with abstracting, which is a part of comprehending and expressing thought. The diagram shown in Figure 6-1 will aid the student in locating the actual level of abstraction and provide him with valuable feedback as to where his own interpretation is located. This will give him a better feeling for abstracting. Two exercises will serve as illustrations here.

Exercise 6.5   *The Meaning of Proverbs*

Two exercises in this category can be used: (1) translating a proverb by moving horizontally in order to give the student a better base for his later attempts at abstracting, and (2) translating vertically by pulling away from the original statement on the concrete level and reaching for higher levels of conceptualization. In the first instance, the student might find that "An apple a day keeps the doctor away" means pretty much the same thing as "A stitch in time saves nine." Or he may make his own translations, like "Going to the doctor for a checkup might prevent bigger trouble or illness later on." The examples given in Figure 6-2 might be used initially.

Exercise 6.6   *Class Inclusions and Exclusions*

This exercise is related to classification tasks previously mentioned, except that similarities and differences of word concepts are used. The student is asked to pick out the one word that does *not belong* there. Another version calls for words which *all* fall into one category and the student is again asked to name the category. What is required here is to abstract from the concrete meaning of the words the higher conceptual levels through classifying according to similarities and differences—i.e., the supra-class.

a. Which word does *not* belong in this group?

horse   pig   sow   cow   fork   bird   (Answer: fork)
airplane   boat   taxi   tire   bus   cruiser   (Answer: tire)

b. What do these words have in common?

chair table dresser stool sofa (Answer: furniture)
etymology syntax phonology lexicology (Answer: Linguistics, the Science of Language)
chalk   paper   pen   pencil   stick   (Answer: writing)

Summarizations

Some students have difficulty separating the essential from the nonessential which may be related to the figure-ground phenomenon; i.e., they cannot bring essential features of a story into focus without being distracted by the background or irrelevant information. This condensing process may be part of a person's "cognitive sytle," but if the student has difficulty with this aspect of learning, appropriate exercises can be selected to strengthen his weakness.

Figure 6-2

Levels of Abstraction in Proverbs and Sayings

Literal Example	Examples of Low Level of Abstraction	Examples of Higher Level of Abstraction
Where there is smoke, there is fire.	Since fires usually have smoke, you can guess that there is a fire when you see smoke.	Cause and effect.
A man driven by distress does as much as 30.	If you are scared, you can do a lot more than you might think you could.	The intensity of the action depends on the strength of the motive.
You can't make an omelet without breaking eggs.	If you want to do something, some damage may be necessary.	To succeed, you must be willing to disregard obstacles. Start at the beginning.
One must leave a room by door and window.	We must leave by the way we came in. Don't try the unusual, it won't work!	Conventionalism or conformity.
Make hay while the sun shines.	Get things inside the house or barn while you can.	Take advantage of an opportunity.
The greatest river runs into the sea.	All rivers and brooks eventually end in the ocean.	Destiny
The sick man sleeps when the debtor cannot.	If your mind is troubled, you will be restless.	Conscience
The fruit never falls far from the tree.	Fruits, like apples or peaches, always are gathered near the trees they grow on.	Heredity or origin.

Figure 6-2 (cont'd.)

		Mastery
In the hands of a good shot, every rifle is deadly.	If you are good at shooting, you always hit the bullseye.	Personal involvement guarantees execution of demands.
If you want a thing done, go; if not, send!	Better do it yourself if you want things done.	
Sugar itself may spoil a good dish.	Don't overdue even the good ingredients for a dish.	Too much of anything is bad. There is even a limit to goodness.
He that helps another helps himself.	You feel better if you help someone else.	Helping actions reflect on the giver.
No fine clothes can hide the clown.	Make-up doesn't hide a foolish man.	There is no cover-up for foolishness.
Old praise dies unless you feed it.	Don't praise just once!	Praise has to be a continuous giving of rewards.
The fairest-looking shoe may pinch the foot.	Even though it's a fine-looking shoe, take it off if it hurts you.	Outward appearance can be deceiving.
The bait hides the hook.	Watch out for the hook, even though it has goodies wrapped around it.	Evil is wrapped in desire.
Half a loaf is better than none.	Consider yourself lucky if you have something to eat.	Be satisfied with what you have.
Try the ice before you venture on it.	Don't step on thin ice; you might have an accident.	Precautions must be taken before daring actions.
Walls have ears.	Watch out when you talk, someone might listen in.	If you want seclusion, make sure it's safe!

Exercise 6.7 *Paragraph Reading*

The student and teacher read a paragraph aloud together. Be sure that the level of the text is appropriate for his reading development. At the end of the reading, ask him to summarize the meaning of the entire paragraph by using only a few words. You might say: "Here are four or five blanks. Can you fill them with words?" Paragraphs should be carefully selected, keeping the purpose of the exercise in mind.

Exercise 6.8 *Newspaper Reporter*

We proceed with the exercise as in 6.7, except that the student is asked to pretend that he is a newspaper reporter and must call in his "headline" to the central office downtown. He is again allowed four or five blanks to make his headline. If he does not succeed, a correct solution might be given for the first few times, or leading questions may be asked which direct the student's attention to the essentials of the summarization.

Exercise 6.9 *Newspaper Reporter (Oral Version)*

Some students may have difficulty in reading simple stories but may still need experience in summarizing. In such instances, and as a preparatory exercise for reading and written work, the student can be given the story orally. After carefully listening to the story (perhaps about an accident or a fire), the student then "reports" the headline. A collection of stories can be kept on prerecorded tape, filed for easy use. The stories should contain both relevant and irrelevant information so that the student is required to sift out the main ideas to be included in the final headline. The task can be increased in difficulty by reducing the number of words in the headline, say from five or six in the beginning, to three or four at the end. Difficulty level can be varied by using shorter or longer stories.

Opposites

Opposites help teach thinking and comprehension by exploring the extremes of a given word or dimension, like hot and cold, left and right, sweet and sour, or calm and excited. The difficulty level of these opposites can be increased as the student gains in proficiency.

Exercise 6.10   *What's the Opposite of ???*

(Easy task)   (More difficult task)

under _____   shy   _____
wrong _____   restless _____
pretty _____   straight _____
tall _____   bold   _____
hard _____   clumsy _____
cold _____   harmless _____
quick _____   clever   _____

Metaphors

Exercises in metaphoric expressions likewise give the student a good chance to express himself and his thoughts in many different, often not only abstract but also creative ways. We distinguish between fixed and flexible metaphors and give the student a number of exercises in each of these two categories to increase his comprehension and abstracting facility.

Exercise 6.11   *Fixed and Frozen Metaphors*

Some metaphors are called frozen or fixed metaphors. They are of the conventional variety. The second variety is called flexible or novel.

Examples:	Examples:
(fixed)	(flexible)
Daily Bread	Bombs rained over London.
Way of Life	The brass-like sound of his
In Apple Pie Order	voice trumpeted in the dark.

Can you add to these lists?

Exercise 6.12   *Make Metaphors of Your Own*

Ask the student to make up metaphors of his own, giving certain conditions or situations as a base. You may also ask him to underline metaphors in his reading exercises.

Setting: Two girls are walking by while you are sitting on a bench in the park.
You like the girls, they appeal to you, especially the way they walk past you.

Example: The girls looked like Madonnas out of Botticelli.
The two drew my attention like meatballs do on Ma's spaghetti.
I felt as if I had been struck by lightning when I looked into their gleaming eyes.

Drawing Generalizations from Pictures

In order to assist the student in going beyond concrete levels of thinking to higher levels of abstraction and concept formation, pictures (slides or photographs) are shown to him. These pictorial clues can be cut out of magazines or other resource material. Examples are displayed in Photo 6-2 through Photo 6-4. It is important that the student be instructed to give the picture an appropriate title, but in as high an abstraction as possible. Generalizing the picture in Photo 6-2, for instance, "My dog" is a literal meaning of the picture. Generalizing it to "Companion" or "Man's Best Friend" would be better, meaning that it is a higher abstraction.

For practice in generalizing meaning from pictorial clues, try the following:

Exercise 6.13   *Picture of a dog with its generalizations of alertness or friendship. (See Photo 6-2.) Use pictures of different animals.*

Photo 6-2

Concrete Level   My Dog
                                  A Dog Sitting Down
                                  Man's Best Friend
                                  A Companion
                                  Watchfulness
                                  On Guard
                                  Companionship
                                  Alertness
                                  Contentment
Abstract Level   Friendship

Exercise 6.14   *Picture of a target, with generalizations of sportsmanship or mastery. (See Photo 6-3.) Try other pictures of sports equipment and see what you can get.*

Photo 6-3

Concrete   Target
                           Bull's Eye
                           Hit
                           Sport
                           Archery
                           Achievement
                           Goal
                           Aim
                           Center
                           Mastery
Abstract   Sportsmanship

Exercise 6.15   *Picture of an aged woman with a baby,
                     with generalizations of tranquillity or
                     security (See Photo 6-4.) Try other pictures
                     showing different kinds of people,
                     tradesmen, soldiers, or professionals.*

Photo 6-4

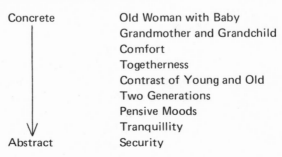

Concrete	Old Woman with Baby
	Grandmother and Grandchild
	Comfort
	Togetherness
	Contrast of Young and Old
	Two Generations
	Pensive Moods
	Tranquillity
Abstract	Security

Cause and Effect

Sharp thinking and comprehending can be improved by relating cause and effect. We already encountered this in our exercise with proverbs where the saying "Where there's smoke, there's fire" means cause and effect. Another way of practicing this aspect of thinking is to give the student the cause only, or the effect only, and let him complete the statement. While the exercises with opposites were aimed at finding extremes, cause-and-effect exercises aim more at relationships or relatedness. Analogies aim at similar responses.

Exercise 6.16   *Give Me the Cause for . . . !*
                                 Give Me the Effect of . . . !

If I say *explosion,* what do you say?
If I say *theft,* what do you say?
If I say *accident,* what do you say?
If I say *hunger,* what do you say?

Exercise 6.17   *Analogies*

Gas is related to a car, as food is related to _____ .

Scissors are to paper as an ax might be to a _____ .

Seed is to fruit as an idea is to an _____ .
A finger is related to a hand as a toe is to a _____ .

Vocabulary Clusters

Many poor readers show deficiencies in vocabulary. A good knowledge of words helps the reader to recognize and comprehend what he reads. The more frequently the reader sees familiar words in the text, the quicker he reads and understands what he read. Poor readers often try to *guess* words from context, only to guess wrong and miss the meaning of a given sentence. A new word should be introduced at the beginning of each reading session. Give the definition of the word and cite examples for its usage. Select words that are appropriate to the student's intelligence and grade level, but try to pick high-interest words from among your students' experiential background and culture. The following two exercises will be helpful in building up a treasury of words.

Exercise 6.18   *Word Clusters*

Clusters of words, related to each other but not necessarily as grammatical word families, are written on 3 x 5 cards and displayed on the bulletin board. Each day as the week progresses, an additional word is added which fits into the cluster. Students may choose to do this work themselves with the aid of a dictionary and approval from the teacher.

Parts of a Car	Tools	Professions and Occupations
carburetor	hammer	plumber
accelerator	wrench	bricklayer
pedal	ax	barber
hood	hatchet	doctor
horn	pliers	judge
clutch	saw	janitor
windshield wiper	drill	teacher

Instead of listing words by category or classification, whole word families can be collected that show structural similarities in a variety of ways:

Exercise 6.19

Suffixes Alike	Root or Stem Alike	Prefix Alike
party	operation	conclude
groovy	operator	converse
healthy	operate	construct
tiny	operable	constrict
angry	operating	condemn
happy		conduct
		concentrate

Chapter Summary

Among poor readers are individuals who have mastered word analysis skills, but who are unable to comprehend what they have read. These "word callers" may amaze educators and parents alike by being able to say the words; but when asked questions about the material they read, they are unable to give even simple answers. While comprehension is closely related to cognitive processes or "thinking," it is also considered part of the reading process. One must understand what is being read beyond the concrete, literal meaning of the text in order to make inferences or come to conclusions.

This chapter provides exercises which help the poor reader to understand what he has read. One of the basic requirements in reading is the ability to abstract, to think on higher conceptual levels. While conceptual thinking is closely related to intelligence, specific comprehension skills can be taught. Through appropriate exercises the student can be shown how to abstract, thus deriving richer and fuller meaning from the material he has read. The ultimate goal of reading must not be word recognition skills alone, but the ability to use the meaning of words and sentences, as well.

7

Organizing and Planning Remedial Reading Programs

What are the possibilities open to a student who has failed to acquire reading skills in a regular setting? Should he leave the school system? Get additional help within the system? Should he seek assistance outside the familiar setting? Is he doomed to failure? These are grave questions for someone who has a reading disability, and the questions might be even more painful for someone who calls himself a father or mother, a teacher or tutor.

Many schools and communities faced with older problem readers today lack sufficient resources, both financial and physical, to help these young people in distress. Some school systems do not exert adequate effort to help older poor readers, while others simply do not have the know-how and initiative to build special programs. Yet, the steps to be taken in the right direction are relatively simple, once the decision is made to set up remedial programs. Existing facilities can be used for classrooms or meeting centers, and funding can be avoided by recruiting an active volunteer corps. The leaders or steering committee members need not be teachers or experts. What is needed at the outset are people with persuasive leadership qualities and initiative. When professional assistance is required it can be obtained from community sources, possibly on a part-time basis.

The chart shown in Figure 7-1 will give the reader an overview of available strategies and resources that can be followed singly or in combination. A survey of existing needs based on the extent of the problem should precede the selection of the strategic approaches which can most effectively serve the older poor readers in particular schools and communities.

It is obvious, then, that we must consider the many different approaches to remediation that are available. Often a combination of *several* approaches can be designed to meet the poor reader's specific needs.

IN-SCHOOL APPROACHES

1. Modified Curriculum

By Modified Curriculum is meant a tailor-made plan for a given student or group in need of remedial help. The approach is considered "mainstreaming" because the student remains in the regular curricular program but receives special help outside of the classroom. For example, if a student is especially weak in reading, he might receive individual tutoring in this subject for an hour or two daily. However, for the remainder of his class schedule he stays with his peers and is "mainstreamed." At other times, special arrangements are made with his regular content teachers; e.g., administering all tests *orally* if the student is unable to take written tests because of the severity of his reading problem. Older students are particularly sensitive to

Figure 7-1

Basic Strategies for Helping the Older Poor Reader

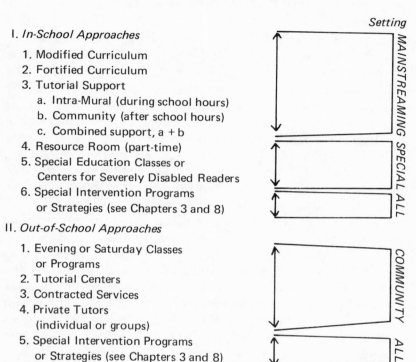

Setting

I. *In-School Approaches*

   1. Modified Curriculum
   2. Fortified Curriculum
   3. Tutorial Support
      a. Intra-Mural (during school hours)
      b. Community (after school hours)
      c. Combined support, a + b
   4. Resource Room (part-time)
   5. Special Education Classes or
      Centers for Severely Disabled Readers
   6. Special Intervention Programs
      or Strategies (see Chapters 3 and 8)

II. *Out-of-School Approaches*

   1. Evening or Saturday Classes
      or Programs
   2. Tutorial Centers
   3. Contracted Services
   4. Private Tutors
      (individual or groups)
   5. Special Intervention Programs
      or Strategies (see Chapters 3 and 8)

MAINSTREAMING SPECIAL ALL

COMMUNITY ALL

the embarrassment of being different and could be helped in this way.

Remember that the poor reader needs a break after keeping his nose to the educational grindstone for prolonged and fatiguing periods. Assigning a student to a double period of remedial reading is one thing, but one cannot assume reading gains will accrue commensurate with the time the individual invests in class. There is a limit to these gains, governed by the law of diminishing returns. There might not be any difference in gain between spending four and spending five hours per day in a remedial reading class. But once the student has recuperated from one remedial hour, he may well take up the reading mallet later in the day and hammer away at it again. Consistent work on a systematic basis is to be preferred over protracted periods of tutoring.

Another way of assisting poor readers in the Modified Curriculum program is by employing the "Pal System" where two students of either the same or different academic levels are paired for the purpose of tutoring each other. A more capable boy might help a poor reader with his reading, under supervision of a remedial reading teacher or a member of the faculty. Sessions can be held during the study period once a day, at specified times during the day, during the regular class session, or even after school hours. If a student consistently fails mathematics because he cannot read the text accompanying the problems, a good reader can be assigned to assist him with the reading part of the problems. It might just turn out that our problem reader, indeed, knows how to solve math problems once the text is read to him.

Allowing students to bring tape recorders into the classroom and giving them permission to record certain parts of the teacher's lecture or oral assignments and explanations also has an important part in the Modified Curriculum. Still another example is having textbooks read into a tape or cassette recorder by someone else, such as a capable student or a volunteer, and making these inexpensive recordings available to the poor reader. What he did not learn through his eyes he has an opportunity to learn through his ears by listening attentively to the recordings while following the text.

2. Fortified Curriculum

The Fortified Curriculum in the regular high school program is similar to the modified one, except that certain aspects of the student's deficiencies, such as figure-ground confusion, are directly and centrally attacked. While in the Modified Curriculum certain remedial strategies are built in on a regular basis, in the Fortified Curriculum we have a place for intensive or "crash" programs which do not necessarily last throughout the school year. Specific needs are met with specific programs or modules, for one single student or for a small group with similar academic problems.

In the Modified Curriculum, attempts are made to minimize difficulties for the student with reading problems by allowing him to be tutored, take tests orally, or receive help from the volunteer tutor on a regular basis. We try to help him survive in a regular program. On the other hand, the Fortified Curriculum tries to attack a given weakness squarely by offering immediate and specific remediation. The student is still mainstreamed and in a regular program. He may conceivably be in a Modified Curriculum program but receive extra help, such as temporary group counseling or perceptual-motor training, in the Fortified Curriculum. These combined approaches are usually even more effective than single ones.

3. Tutorial Support

a. *In-School Support*

It is often claimed that regular classroom teachers cannot teach children with learning disabilities, even if they knew how, because 25 or 30 other children in the room demand the teacher's attention at the same time. While this point could certainly be argued, the fact is that few teachers can do this job without some form of special training. However, students can be tutored individually, outside of the regular class, and thus get the vital instructions and remediation they otherwise would fail to receive.

One of the most effective approaches to individual tutoring is a student-to-student system whereby a good reader, in whatever grade, teaches a poor reader. This approach is equally effective and successful at all levels, elementary through senior high school. Guidance counselors or homeroom teachers can serve as coordinators by making up schedules for the various locations and pairing off tutors with poor readers. Limited space may appear to pose a big problem, but there are nooks and crannies in most schools which are not used for worthwhile purposes during certain hours of the day. The auditorium is not in constant use, the basement might have some semi-private corners, or the school yard might have to do on good weather days.

Distraction-free environments are to be preferred. Frequently, simple blinds or screens can be used to create a less distractive area on the yard or in some corners of a hallway. Large sheets of cardboard can serve this purpose, and the art department might help to enhance their attractiveness. Of course, Fire Department regulations would have to be observed when using hallways.

Paid paraprofessionals are of great help in monitoring these tutorial sessions in a buddy system, but this type of personnel is usually available only when federally funded. The idea of bringing volunteers from the community into the picture is discussed later in more detail. Volunteers can extend the arms of professional personnel immeasurably. Some school systems utilize reading supervisors or consultants to direct the initial phases of in-service training for tutors and aides.

b. *Community Support*

It can be stated that teaching reading is everybody's job. The job of nurturing the desire to read should not be considered the exclusive domain of the professional teacher. If the current level of literacy is to be raised for everyone, teachers and librarians must learn to "spin off" small bits of their knowledge and skill by training others to take over some aspects of their job. Employment of voluntary and paid aides in our schools has proven that these workers are very capable adjunct personnel in the educative process, especially as tutors on a one-to-one basis, while the Master Teacher continues to cater to the needs of the entire class. And the job of remediation cannot be done within the four walls of the school. The poor reader needs outside support as well, 24 hours a day, 'round the clock.

Since educational intervention combined with parapro-fessional tutelage are the two most effective means by which a poor reader can be taught efficiently and inexpensively, the community support approach to tutoring has found ever increasing acceptance among parents and community groups. Resources for tutors are limitless: We can try to locate teenagers living in the neighborhood, members of church groups and civic organizations in town, parents willing to teach other people's children, college students, retired teachers, senior citizens, members of service clubs and women's groups—an endless variety of human energy is yet untapped. This energy can be quickly organized if the need is made known to them. In one city, 22 different civic organizations have combined their efforts under the umbrella of a Council on Learning Disabilities for even more effective operations. They have an answering service at night where desperate parents and anyone else can find resources and names of professionals and programs to help their poor readers. Some school systems have programs for tutors who, after a certain amount of training time, receive a certificate attesting to their qualification as trained learning aides.

c. *Combined Approach*

Best results may be obtained by combining outside and school efforts. The teacher, reading specialist, or resource person in the school may outline a master program which identifies specific assignments to be implemented by a tutor. These assignments can be programmed and structured, in order to offer maximum guidance to the tutorial corps working under the direction of the head teacher in the school. Such programming will be described at the end of this chapter.

4. Resource Room

The idea of a Resource Room was started when it was realized that expensive materials for remedial reading cannot be supplied to everyone in the school because of the high costs involved. In charge of this Resource Room we usually find a specially trained teacher with a strong background in reading, special education, and learning disabilities. The room should be accessible within the building so that everyone can take advantage of the specialized equipment and materials it contains. It should be equipped with a wide variety of reading material, especially the high-interest, low readability kind which appeals to the older poor readers. The room might also house specialized machines such as tachistoscopes, overhead projectors, film-strip projectors, and programmed electronic machines. For the student who is in need of auditory or visual perceptual training there might be materials suitable for a variety of exercises, such as a balance beam, blocks, puzzles, trampoline, and related resource materials. Paid paraprofessionals and volunteers can be of great help to the resource room teacher because most instruction is on an individual basis.

After the student with a reading problem has been identified by the classroom teacher, has been properly studied and diagnosed by a team of professionals, and has had the needed educational prescription determined for 'the remediation of his problem, he should be referred to the Resource Teacher for a pre-determined schedule for part of the day. For example, he might be taken out of his regular classroom for a period of 30 minutes or a full hour on a daily basis in order to receive specialized help from the Resource Teacher. Flexibility of scheduling should be maintained. In this way the student can benefit from the regular curriculum, while receiving specialized help. He is exposed to the atmosphere of a regular classroom, including the friendship of his classmates, and retains his position in the mainstream without being ostracized or labeled. This approach also helps to alleviate secondary emotional reactions which might develop into behavior problems if not recognized and treated. The student is not permanently isolated as he often is in a Special Education class or program, and there is an opportunity to carefully measure his progress. After the student has spent a sufficient length of time in the Resource Room program, he can gradually be reintegrated into the full mainstream, with perhaps only occasional visits to the Resource Room.

Having a Resource Room and its staff available appeals especially to older poor readers because they feel a need to retreat from the regular classroom where they have encountered problems. The Resource Teacher serves as a counselor as well. A brief talk with an aide or volunteer may strengthen the student's confidence to the point where he is once again ready to face the day, when otherwise he might have given up completely or invoked some defense mechanism such as stomach cramps or headache. The Resource Room can be a Sanctuary to the older student who associates the regular classroom with failure.

Photo 7-1

The Resource Room is equipped as a laboratory center for reading. Here a student operates the tachistoscope.

5. Special Education Classes

In cases of severe learning disabilities, the Resource Room will not be adequate to meet the needs because of the severity and depth of the reading problem. In such instances, the student must be transferred to a Special Education program. He is removed from the mainstream and assigned to a special program which offers intensive remediation. Usually, such programs are of long-term duration; some last for several years. At the end of his stay in the Special Education program, the student will be reintegrated into the regular curriculum. Care must be exercised to prepare the receiving classroom teacher with regard to the special needs of the incoming student. Otherwise, reintegration may be a "shock" to the student and he may revert to old symptoms and tactics. The Resource Room may be of great help in this return to the regular setting, allowing the student to spend some time during the day with the Resource Room teacher in order to make the transition smoother and more gradual.

While in the past a transfer to a Special Education program was usually connected with a physical transfer from one school building to another, current trends provide for Special Education classrooms within the regular school. This set-up facilitates separation and reintegration to and from special programs. The purpose of "mainstreaming," as it is called in education, has as its underlying philosophy the idea that handicapped children are "normal" in many ways and should be taught in the least restrictive environment. No hard research data are available on this trend.

OUT-OF-SCHOOL APPROACHES

1. Evening and Saturday Classes

For the student who is still enrolled in school, resources for remediation of learning disabilities are usually available even though they may be limited in scope. The real tragedy sets in once the student is no longer part of a formal educational system, be that private or public. Here we are concerned with the large number of people labeled as dropouts, push-outs, school failures, delinquents, or by whatever name they are carried in sad statistical records. The plight of these people has been described in the first chapter. Many of them are still functional illiterates or very poor readers. They have grown physically but not academically. Some have sought alternate solutions to their problems and entered the world of work, usually on a low entry level because of their inability to read the printed word. Some may be functional readers and try to get by, but sooner or later they will have to face the old question of reading when they try to upgrade themselves or are offered promotions.

These older poor readers no longer have the time available they once had, since they usually work from 8 a.m. to 5 p.m. This limits their available free time to the evening hours or weekends. Others might have found that nightshift work is the only employment they can get. They must sleep during the hours other people use to learn. Still others work odd hours on a part-time basis, never knowing when they will be called to work. Thus the availability of remedial programs presents a real problem for them. Evening or Saturday classes are now the only ones they can attend, which definitely limits their choice of programs. Tutorial Centers, described below, must open their doors during these prime times, keeping in mind that once a person has left the formal school setting, daytime hours are rarely available for the secondary road to learning.

2. Tutorial Centers

Tutorial Centers absorb the type of clientele for whom public school facilities are no longer conveniently available even though the centers may come under the administration of public school systems. They function best with a small nucleus of trained teachers and a large group of aides and volunteer tutors.

A Tutorial Center should be centrally located so that it is easily accessible. In larger urban areas, satellite centers can be opened up in several parts of the community. Organization and physical set-up can parallel those of Resource Rooms. Materials should have appeal to students of older ages. Along with reading instruction, counseling and vocational guidance are extremely important supplements. Many of the participants in Tutorial Centers will upgrade their reading skills, and become eligible for better jobs. Close relationships with the business community are, therefore, also essential. The Centers are usually headed by a Supervisor or Director. To facilitate good relations with the community, an Advisory Council should be formed which consists of leaders in the various community fields. Once these community leaders know about the purpose of the Center, they can be instrumental in promoting and contributing to its success.

3. Contracted Services

Both profit and nonprofit organizations now offer specialized services on a contract basis in schools and other educational settings. Some of these contracting agencies have formed private companies, while others are operating in connection with colleges and universities. The primary advantage of securing the services of outside contractors lies in the fact that expensive mistakes can be avoided by employing the know-how and experience of people who have run similar enterprises before. The contracted services usually include in-service training for teachers and volunteers and often extend to materials, equipment, and evaluation procedures. The trainers who initially implement the program retire after the program is operable and return only for intermittent evaluations. Some companies sell only the blueprint, while others get involved in the actual process of teaching and managing. Federal, state, and local agencies are frequently able to supply names of individuals or companies which provide contractual services. Local colleges and universities offer similar help through their Education Department. The question of federal and state funding of Tutorial Centers is also worth exploring with the aforementioned agencies. As would be true in any outside contract work, care must be exercised to secure qualified and reliable people. Unfortunately, there have been some expensive failures through these contracted services.

4. Home Tutors

By far the most convenient and tailor-made way of supplying tutors is to hire their services on an individual basis. Professional tutors now charge anywhere from $4 to $15 per hour depending on the academic background of the tutor and the geographic location. It is obvious that such tutorial services cannot be afforded by everyone, but they are the most effective way of starting a tutorial program immediately, without going through the pains of searching for an appropriate school or clinic and paying registration fees and other incidental costs. The home tutor may follow his own strategy of remediation or he may be given directions and educational prescriptions by a professional who previously diagnosed the reading problem or evaluated the student's level of performance. Costs for tutoring can be reduced by transporting the student to the tutor's home, or by forming small groups of students with similar problems. If a pool of tutors can be gathered by a coordinating organization or parent affiliation, very fine tutorial programs can be established at a relatively small cost.

5. Special Intervention Programs

The special intervention programs and strategies listed at the end of Sections I and II in Figure 7-1 in the beginning of the chapter are ancillary or supplementary to the basic approaches used in schools and communities. For example, so-called programmed approaches may be employed with built-in provisions for immediate rewards at the end of a small segment of work. Behavior modification techniques are now widely employed in connection with remedial work in order to reinforce success and minimize failure. The same techniques may be used to manage small groups more effectively and keep discipline problems to a minimum and work time to a maximum. Another program effective for the poor reader and from which he can benefit is a counseling service. Some of these programs and techniques have been described in Chapter 3 and will be further dealt with in Chapter 8. The reader may also refer to the Appendix where further references are given.

DEVELOPING A REMEDIAL MASTER PLAN

Once the objectives for tutorial intervention have been established on the basis of student needs and a careful diagnostic assessment, it becomes necessary to devise a list of specific performance objectives which can be considered the master plan from which all individual lesson plans can be derived.

The Behavioral Objectives, as they are called in educational jargon, have to be established first. What is to be accomplished in the remedial program? Is the student to be helped generally to catch up with his present class level, or must he be singled out for a more incisive remedial instruction? Next we derive from the broad objectives the more specific ones, the Performance Objectives, as they are called, which give directions on means of accomplishment. If the student shows severe and numerous reversal errors in his reading, what remedial exercises must we employ and what can be reasonably expected from him within a specified time span? This is where the master plan comes in.

The master plan guarantees that the student will be taught according to diagnosed needs. It provides the teacher or tutor with the necessary structure of sequential blueprints for individual sessions. It progresses from the broad, overall objectives and goals to the specific details, ending in so-called modules. A carefully structured organization and construction of these modules is essential to a systematic approach in tutorial remediation. If such plans are not made, waste and repetition may result.

Suggestions for master plans in remedial instruction follow. The approach provides large categories first, which are then segmented into subheadings, and eventually spelled out in an actual lesson. Once the master plan is established and made available to the teacher, she can develop her own curricular plans based on available modules. The suggestions given here are merely examples and may be set up differently to meet the needs of schools and individuals. The master plan is essentially a retrieval system that is not confined to use with reading instructions. Such a system can be adapted to other subjects as well. The plans offered here are incomplete and intended only to demonstrate the basic idea.

A.   *Basic Master Plan*

Category	Examples
A.1 Phonetic Word Attack Skills	A.11 Initial positions (*c*at)
	A.12 Medial positions (tea*s*ing)
Consonants	A.13 Final positions (ben*d*)
	A.14 Blends (ch, bl, cr,)
	A.15 Single (short, long)
	A.16 Double (diphthongs and
Vowels	digraphs)
	A.17 Phonograms (c-AT)

A.2 Visual Recognition	A.21	Alphabet (printed)
Single Letters	A.23	Affixes
Words		Stems or Roots
		Prefixes
		Suffixes
	A.24	Families (familiar roots)
Word Clusters	A.25	Tachistoscopic Work (flash
Speed		cards)
A.3 Comprehension	A.31	Vocabulary Building (mean-
Single Words		ing of words)
	A.32	Synonyms, Homonyms, Anto-
Word Categories		nyms.
	A.33	Paragraph Summaries
Sentences		Predicting Outcomes
		Propaganda
		Interpretive Moods, etc.
	A.34	Author's Style
Enrichment	A.35	Etymologies
	A.36	Words of Foreign Origin
	A.37	High-Frequency Word Counts,
		etc.

B. *Master Plan for Learning Disabilities* (Examples Only)

Sample Category	Examples		Exercise or Task	
B.1 Sensory-Motor	B.12	Gross	B.121	Throwing ball
	B.13	Fine	B.128	Holding Pencil (tracing)
	B.21	Auditory	B.211	Messages with Telegraph Key
B.2 Perceptual	B.22	Visual		
	B.23	Kinesthetic		
	B.24	Olfactory		
	B.25	Tactile		
	B.26	Combinations	B.269	Tracing letters on sandpaper with finger
B.3 Orientation in Space	B.31	Concept High-Low		
	B.32	Concept Left-Right	B.321	Drawing lines from left to right, with color-coded margins (l=green=Go!) (r=red=Stop!)
B.4 Visual Memory	B.41	Visual Memory	B.411	Recall of objects, increas-
	B.42	Auditory Memory		ing in number, by look- ing at displays
B.5 Sequencing	B.51	Ordering words		
	B.52	Ordering objects		
	B.53	Ordering events	B.531	Arranging a series of mixed- up pictures

The sample plans given above are not complete systems but merely serve to demonstrate what categories might have to be considered in a system. Code numbers may be systematically assigned to the various categories and subcategories for easy classification and quick retrieval, but this systematic approach would probably go beyond the task of an individual teacher, even though a school system or clinic would want to consider such a master plan.

DEVELOPING LESSON MODULES

The entire master plan can be "programmed" on individual cards representing lesson segments. Each card or unit contains information about the subcategory, which is either spelled out in detail or shows examples from which the teacher can select tasks. Each module should be designed to provide approximately 15 minutes of tutoring. In this way the teacher is able to build a tutorial session composed of multiple tasks clustering around the topic to be remediated, while offering a variety of planned approaches. Approximately four different modules would constitute a session, usually lasting for one hour.

The composition of modules can be made sequential; i.e., four tasks of increasing difficulty within the same subcategory can be contained in one lesson or offered during subsequent sessions. Modular planning assures continuity of teaching a certain subject. For example, four modules on auditory discrimination can be combined in one session, or one or two segments can be offered together with another task the student needs. A special module for "counseling" or "emoting" may be interspersed in the sequence to allow for consideration of emotional reactions connected with the learning problem. A sample module is offered here.

EXPLANATION OF MODULE COMPONENTS

The following sample module contains the subheadings that will be followed in the subsequent discussion.

MODULE CODE: 05-003-012

GENERAL AREA: Phonetic Training

OBJECTIVE: Mastery of words containing triple consonants (consonantal clusters)

MATERIALS: 3 x 5 cards with short sample words and
sample words embedded in short sentences.

TIME: 10-15 min.

SAMPLE TASK: *scr*oll, r*isks, spr*awl, *scr*amble
Scribes are afraid of scrolls.

RESOURCE: Wagner, R., *Teaching Phonics with Success,* Mafex Associates, Johnstown, Pa.,
1960.

EVALUATION:

The Module Code

The coding system is designed to categorize the various
exercises and file them systematically so that retrieval can occur
quickly and efficiently. The system need not be a complex one,
nor does it have to be complete in the beginning. Its primary
purpose is to provide a skeleton outline that allows "slots" for
future growth and development of the system as needed. Each
exercise or module card, as illustrated above, is labeled at the
top with a specific code number indicating exactly the category
of the exercise, a subarea, and other pertinent information to be
used in planning a complete curriculum or an individual
tutoring session. For example, a code number 02-004-113
indicates in one system that we are dealing with the perceptual
category (02), olfactory topical area (004), and a given subarea
exercise (113) involving the smelling sense, such as smelling
extracts in jars and then attempting to read the labels on the
jars. As long as a skeleton outline is prepared in advance and a
file system is designed, modules can be added as they become
available by simply classifying them and including them in the
existing system of modules. The format as shown on this page

should be followed as closely as possible for the sake of uniformity.

General Area (Topic)

This heading on the module card will serve as a quick reference label and indicates specifically the area in which the remedial training is offered. A student may need strengthening of his skills in a specific area, or he may need remediation in the entire topical area; e.g., phonetic training or visual-perceptual training. With adolescent and adult poor readers, complete coverage of one area might often not be possible or advisable, but certain aspects of phonetic training might be selected, like consonantal blends which give the poor reader trouble. Some of the other topical areas to be included are:

Vocabulary Building
Word Structure
Sentence Structure
Word Origins
Quick Word Recognition
Speed Reading
Comprehension

Objective

Objectives must be stated in a clear language so that every tutor using the module system will know exactly and precisely what the purpose of the modular exercise is. These objectives, also referred to as *Performance Objectives* when specified in terms of what the student has to *do,* spell out what the student must accomplish through a given task or exercise. For example, in our sample module, the task is learning triple consonantal blends embedded in words such as *scr*ipt or *str*eet. The same module may have to be presented repeatedly if the student does not reasonably master the task in one session.

Materials

Under this card heading, the needed materials for the

modular task are listed so that the teacher can be prepared in advance. Material may include paper and pencil, or it may include scissors, crayons, or specific worksheets. These hints for needed material can become most valuable when substitute teachers have to take over on short notice and would otherwise be unprepared and confused. Substitute teachers/tutors are simply handed the module card which contains specific instructions. This provides for increased uniformity of teaching.

Time

While this heading is self-explanatory, some tasks may require longer drills or sessions. On the average, it is advisable to make all modular units uniform with regard to time, but time spans ranging anywhere from five to 20 minutes are tolerated by the system. Four to five modules constitute a tutorial session in order to allow for flexibility and shifts in attention. Modules may be timed according to the student's motivation and interest span. A student with a short attention span needs more modules at first in order to provide for more frequent changes of scenery, while mature adults could possibly continue with only two to three such shifts.

Sample Task

After the objective of the task or exercise has been specified in general behavioral terms, the heading of Sample Task is intended to describe an example of a task or list several possibilities. If larger cards are used for the modules the space for this heading might be larger, allowing for more detailed descriptions of the exercises. Larger cards also may allow for writing on the reverse side. However, notes under this heading may refer the teacher to a file system where the tasks are kept by code. For example, single worksheets of the Frostig exercises or Sullivan workbooks may be kept in this way for convenient retrieval by the teacher. If only examples are chosen to be included on the module card, they should be representative of what is to be taught during the session. Several examples usually illustrate the exercise better than an explanation. The examples of module cards at the end of this chapter will further illustrate the idea of listing sample tasks.

Resource

Under the resource heading we find references which may give the teacher further possibilities for teaching the module contents. References may be given in the form of articles or books, or hints can be more informal, like referring the teacher to a Reading Clinic in town or a specific bookstore where such materials are available.

Evaluation

The last category is an essential part of the entire module and provides the teacher with some measure of achievement or success. The type of evaluation will vary, of course, according to the nature of the module task. At times, some questions relating to the task content may be used, while in other instances the student might be asked to perform an actual activity. Two examples follow:

Comprehension What did the two boys do after they caught the chicken?

Phonics Can you make two sounds where only the lips move? (b, p)
They are called explosive sounds.

The tutor may also note to what extent a student must perform a task to be considered as "passing" or achieving "reasonable mastery." This achievement level can be expressed in the number of questions correctly answered by the student, by demonstrated ability, or possibly in percentages.

SAMPLE MODULES

The following five module samples will provide the teacher/tutor with some idea how these modules look in actual practice. The variety is large and may be started with a nucleus first, to be expanded as the need arises or as the system proves itself.

A.

MODULE CODE: 07-223-116

GENERAL AREA: Reading for Fun and Enjoyment

OBJECTIVE: Motivating student to read high interest texts and avoid discouragement in academic achievement

MATERIALS: *Popular Mechanics* Magazine, or similar journal

TIME: 10-20 min.

SAMPLE TASK: How to fix a carburetor (article)

RESOURCE: *Popular Mechanics,* June 19___, pp. 33-35.

EVALUATION: Ask student to sketch carburetor and write in parts.
Alternate: Give student sketch of carburetor and ask him to point to parts as given by teacher.

B.

MODULE CODE: 05-319-556

GENERAL AREA: Vocabulary Building

OBJECTIVE: Spelling specific nouns related to cars or engines

MATERIALS: *Popular Mechanics* Magazine

TIME: 10-15 min.

SAMPLE TASK: Ask the student to pick words out of articles in the magazine, some he already knows and some he does not know how to spell (at least 5 in this exercise), and list them on a sheet of paper. Examples: Motor, engine, lights, hood, fan, wheel, handle, etc.

RESOURCE: *PM,* any issue. Library has back numbers in stacks.

EVALUATION: Spell 7 out of 10 words correctly.

C.

MODULE CODE: 06-003-233

GENERAL AREA: Word Origins (vocabulary)

OBJECTIVE: To increase word power through the study of word origins, here German language.

MATERIALS: Card set with word origins (German)

TIME: 10-15 min.

SAMPLE TASK: (given to student in person ORALLY or on tape)   PRETZEL—Folk etymology: Monk in Germany (Italy?) baked bread and taught Latin. Students needed motivation, so monk thought of rewards for them. Had bread dough left over, molded it into long snake-shaped noodle, then folded ends over to make shape of pretzel. Folded ends of dough reminded him of folded arms of students when in prayer, with heads bowed. Latin word for "little reward" is *pretiola* from which *pretzel* is derived.

RESOURCE: Wagner, R. and Wagner, M., *Stories about Words,* J. Weston Walch, Portland, Maine. Also see dictionaries and encyclopedias.

EVALUATION: Illustrate knowledge of origins of three words by drawing sketches on paper.

D.

MODULE CODE: 05-499-341

GENERAL AREA: Building Sight Vocabulary

OBJECTIVE: Sight recognition of words by recognizing structural segments of the word: suffix -ION

MATERIALS: Card set, see files under same code. Slide set (tachistoscope). Newspapers. Red felt-tipped marker.

TIME: 10 minutes

SAMPLE TASK:

attent — ion	Have student copy some of the words he does not know, and underline the suffix (-ion) with red marker. Provide newspaper and ask student to look for words with structural segments just learned.
les — ion	
reg — ion	
leg — ion	
affect — ion	
resurrect — ion	

RESOURCE: None

EVALUATION: Demonstrate ability by underlining structural segments in one paragraph of newspaper, without errors.

E.

MODULE CODE: 08-110-211

GENERAL AREA: Building positive self-image

OBJECTIVE: Engage in discussion with student so that the affective level is tapped after exercises (and possible failures). Provide student with encouragement and positive reinforcement of success.

TIME: 10-15 min., preferably at end of session or after repeated failure

SAMPLE TASK: Ask and discuss, allowing student to react affectively:

1. How did it feel last time you got a failing grade?
2. What could you have done to avoid it?
3. What alternates did you have?
4. What did others in the class do when they got a failing grade?
5. How could you have reacted differently?

RESOURCE: Wm. Glasser, *Reality Therapy* (Harper & Row, NYC), *Schools Without Failure* (same publ.)

EVALUATION: *Active* participation in discussion.

Chapter Summary

Remedial reading activities can be organized by employing basic strategies and varying them to fit individual needs and situations. Programs may include various in-school and out-of-school approaches, and combinations of these. To be effective, remedial programs must be clearly focused and well planned. For this purpose, the chapter presents guidelines for translating goals and performance objectives into a master remedial plan. This plan consists of small units, or "modules." These modules form the nucleus of an effective curriculum for learning-disabled students, especially for older poor readers who may have missed certain segments and phases of the curriculum in the past. An individual tutoring session can consist of several modules to offer intensity or variety to the student. The module structure allows for precise planning and continuity in teaching. The master plan serves as a guarantee and control for precision teaching.

8

Coping with Poor Readers: The Affective Domain

A leading educator in the field of language disabilities in adolescents and adults is Alice Ansara, Head of the Reading Department at Manter Hall School in Cambridge, Massachusetts. In one of her articles dealing with the plight of the reading-disabled adolescent, she states:

"The high school years are also a time of introspection for the adolescent, a time of self-examination and self-doubt even while he is reaching toward the adult world. Thus the 'crisis of identity' and the increasing demands of school combine to make the dyslexic boy and girl especially vulnerable during these crucial years. These young people become discouraged and eventually give up the struggle by becoming drop-outs either within or without the school walls. Frequently also, they express their feelings of anxiety and frustration—even self-hate and guilt—in ways that neither they nor the adults around them understand."[1]

What all this means is that the struggling young people in their quandary need realistic and sensitive counseling. There seems to be no specific person or technique which best suits these needs. A professional counselor can do the job provided that he or she is attuned to the problems facing the poor reader. If the professional counselor is unavailable, a sympathetic teacher, student teacher, parent, or anyone else who is human, alive, and has understanding for the situation must do the job. What needs to be tapped is the affective level of behavior, the area in which feelings and emotions are expressed.

VOCATIONAL COUNSELING AND REHABILITATION NEEDED

Since the older poor reader may not only be worried about his vocational future but may, indeed, encounter obstacles and frustrations in his desperate search for a suitable career, intensive and specialized counseling services in this area are of paramount importance. For the sake of efficiency and economy, such counseling may require the formation of small groups to disseminate information. Another approach is to expose the students to actual work experiences in the community. The student may be allowed to spend a few hours or a whole day with a craftsman, a store manager, or a plant foreman. At other times, these people may be asked to come to the school for talks and demonstrations.

Since the older poor reader can be classified as "handicapped" by definition, he may become eligible for special consideration in federally supported programs such as rehabilitation services. Rehabilitation units can be located by contacting appropriate state agencies, usually listed in the tele-

---

[1] Alice Ansara, "Language Therapy to Salvage the College Potential of Dyslexic Adolescents." *Bulletin of the Orton Society,* XXII, 1972, Reprint No. 48. Quotation reprinted with the permission of the author and of the Society.

phone directory. These units may operate independently within the framework of statewide rehabilitation services, or they may be attached to larger school systems. Usually, adolescents become eligible at the age of 15 but policies may vary in different localities. In some instances, preventive intervention can be started before the specified age of eligibility. Some agencies provide for diagnostic workups only, while others have remedial facilities, again depending on the locality and its regulations.

INTERVENTION AND COPING TECHNIQUES

One way of dealing with the behavior of poor readers is by *directive* intervention. A technique is used by the educator to bring about a desired behavior or eliminate an undesirable behavior. Techniques of this nature are usually referred to as "behavior modification."

Other forms of intervention are less direct: We learn to understand the poor reader's *modus operandi* and, through counseling, help him discover more productive ways of dealing with his problems. We do not "operate" on established behavior patterns directly and no direct intervention takes place. The educator becomes more of a counselor by first trying to get insight into the student's behavioral repertoire, often expressed in "games" he plays, or defense mechanisms developed as means of avoiding painful situations or compensating for failures.

Behavior Modification: A Direct Approach

Behavior modification has its historical roots in the animal experiments of the Russian Ivan Pavlov who conditioned dogs to salivate in response to blinking lights or buzzers which were presented, at first, simultaneously with food, and later, alone. The animals "learned" new responses through these conditioning procedures.

In this country, the name of the eminent psychologist B.F. Skinner is associated with the strong behavior modification movement. While Pavlov's type of conditioning is now referred to as classical or Pavlovian, Skinnerian or operant conditioning methods take different forms.

Skinner takes behavior which already is present in the person's repertoire and tries to either increase the frequency of desirable behavior, or decrease the frequency of occurrence of undesirable behavior. Applied to reading instruction this may mean that we want to increase the amount of time a student spends reading books or increase the number of new words he learns within a given time span. On the other hand, we might want to decrease errors or inattention.

All this is done by what professionals in this field call reinforcement, either positive or negative. Positive reinforcement may take the form of a reward—a gift or a nod or smile from the teacher—while negative reinforcement may consist of losing valuable playtime on the yard when a mistake occurs, or being reprimanded by the teacher.

Behavior modification techniques can be applied to individuals, small groups, whole classes, or school populations. Programs using tokens which may be exchanged for rewards are referred to as token economies. The token may be a small chip or coin which can be exchanged for a reward of a more meaningful nature. References describing the application of behavior modification, or "B.Mod." for short, in various educational settings, are given at the end of the book in the Appendix. Some basic principles are described below.

1. *Reinforcement.* One of the basic principles of behavior modification in the operant-type model is that the reinforcement must be given simultaneously with the behavioral act to be conditioned so that the student can form an associative bond between the behavioral event and the reinforcer. For example, if the student pronounces a newly attacked word correctly and the teacher wishes to reinforce this correct behavior on an operant basis, he or she will offer him a small token, smile, or reward him in other ways immediately. In the contingency-type model, the establishment of the consequences of the student's behavior must be clearly understood and contracted.

Reinforcers can be classified in several ways. One way of categorizing them for convenience is dividing them into VER-

BAL and NONVERBAL which, in turn, can be broken down into two subdivisions of POSITIVE and NEGATIVE, yielding a total of four subgroups:

VERBAL — POSITIVE   ("That's great!")

VERBAL — NEGATIVE   ("No, that's wrong!")

NONVERBAL — POSITIVE   (Teacher pats student on the shoulder or gives a token.)

NONVERBAL — NEGATIVE   (Teacher shows disapproval, retrieves token previously earned, or sends student to "time-out" corner.)

Another way of grouping reinforcers is to classify them according to their forms:

ACTIVITY REINFORCERS allow the student to engage in some form of activity, such as listening to his favorite records, playing in a tree house, or baking cookies. A token may be given out which later can be exchanged for these activities.

MATERIAL OR OBJECT REINFORCERS are most commonly used in behavior modification experiments. Trading stamps, plastic rings, books, pencils, combs, toy soldiers, or other small trinkets are in this group. Again, tokens may be used to postpone the gratification.

PEOPLE REINFORCERS are rewards of time and attention. They are nonmaterial but they rank high in value among students, especially adolescents and adults. They may take place in a social setting such as a peer group or the family. It is the human relationship which is the primary agent of reinforcement.

2. *Scheduling and Programming.* Reinforcements are given on a systematic basis employing regular or irregular intervals. For example, a student may be given additional free time as a reward after finishing a page in the workbook with 80 percent accuracy. As another example, a token may be given to those

students in the class who stay in their seats for a specified period of time during independent work periods. As they gain in the skill of sitting still or remaining in their seats, the teacher may decide to reward only every other behavioral act. If reinforcement is not given every time the behavioral act occurs, but only at a given predetermined sequence, we refer to this type of scheduling as intermittent. It may occur on a fixed or variable schedule of reinforcement.

Reinforcement must not be viewed as a means of "control" over students' performance because it may evoke a feeling of power over an individual or group. Reinforcement should be viewed as a means of increasing motivation leading toward a goal. The technique is particularly suited for older students who have lost interest in academic work and whose motivational drive is at a minimum. The very goal of reading "turns them off." Renewed encouragement must be offered in the form of incentives and rewards. Offering incentives is nothing new to those who have worked in industrial settings. Many types of workers are offered incentives to finish work within a certain time or for producing a desired quantity of goals. Production improves as incentives are given. The same principle can be applied to improve the performance of the older poor reader. The educator must proceed with caution, being careful to use an incentive system as a means of motivating poor readers, rather than as a means of controlling their motivation. The most effective reinforcement takes place when the motivated behavior is self-generated or task-generated; i.e., it either comes from within the student's own attitudinal system and his desire to improve, or is generated from an interesting and exciting task itself.

3. *Design and Evaluation.* Careful planning of the modification technique will guarantee success. Sloppily executed programs are doomed to failure and may not be worth the effort that goes into their planning. A good design includes a pre-modification period; i.e., a period of time when the student's current performance level is observed without offering reinforcements. This pre-modification period is known as the assessment phase or Baseline I, a basis for later evaluative

comparisons. For example, a student may reverse the word "was" in a given text 15 times during a tutorial session, or he may say "No" 25 times during a session in response to the tutor's requests. Having him read the word "was" from left to right, or saying "Yes" in response to the tutor's request, is the desirable behavior we wish to increase in frequency of occurrence.

Once a baseline is established, we are ready to modify the behavior. The length of the modification period depends on the specific behavior we wish to change or alter. Changing a student's behavior to paying attention to the text from not paying attention may be accomplished more quickly than deep-seated activities, such as in-seat behavior or fidgetiness in the classroom. Nobody would expect a student to read complicated words without mistakes the moment a reward is offered by the tutor. Finishing a page in the workbook on time might be easy for one student but difficult for another.

After the modification period, reinforcements may be stopped or gradually diminished. Again, an evaluation takes place in order to determine success. The student's behavior, be that reading words or finishing a page, is again counted, this time without the use of reinforcers. This is referred to as the Second Baseline and it provides a means of comparison between pre- and post-modification periods. If a student was able to finish two pages in three hours during the pre-modification period, but now finishes eight pages during the same time and with 90 percent accuracy (an arbitrarily set goal), the strategy was obviously successful and can actually be specified in numerical terms. Figure 8-1 shows improvement that took place in one student's performance during behavior modification geared to learning new vocabulary.

Measuring the acquisition of new vocabulary is only one example of how "B. Mod." can be applied to remedial reading. There are many other ways of using the technique, such as increasing the number of pages read by a student during homeroom studies, allowing points for comprehension questions at the end of a given reading text, or increasing the time (in minutes) a student focuses on a reading task without

Figure 8-1

Progress Chart for Reading Improvement

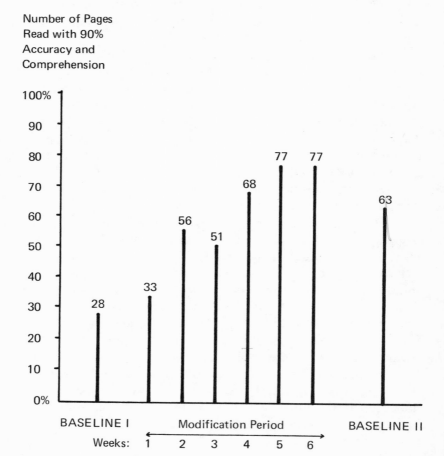

Number of Pages
Read with 90%
Accuracy and
Comprehension

Reinforcer: One token per page read with 90% accuracy and comprehension
Token Exchange: 10 Tokens equal 1 plastic trinket
                 25 Tokens equal 15 minutes extra play time in the yard
                 50 Tokens equal 1 book prize

interruption or distraction. The technique should not be used exclusively over other available methods, nor should it be employed in order to gain control over a given situation without. taking all human and situational variables into consideration. The technique must be used within the broader context of remedial efforts, not in narrow isolation.

Defense Mechanisms: Understanding Indirect Behavior

Any "handicapped" person resorts to all kinds of mechanisms in order to be able to cope with his reactions to the so-called normal human environment. People with reading problems likewise show these emotional reactions. It is wise for the teacher of adolescents with reading problems to know the nature of some of these reactions so that they can be anticipated and understood. The following overview presents a workable grouping of these reactions.

1. *Defense and Avoidance Mechanisms.* The mechanisms in this category are evidenced in specific behavioral acts, such as the pretended or actual loss of a report card or refusal to read due to the pretended or actual loss of glasses. While these defense maneuvers can also be employed by normal persons who try to avoid embarrassing situations, the poor reader may have to take full advantage of the mechanisms in order to preserve self-respect. Adolescents with reading difficulties have learned to avoid any place or situation where reading is a basic requirement. They would rather feel sick than read a paragraph in front of their classmates.

2. *Compensatory Mechanisms.* The mechanisms in this category show a change in behavior. This change is an attempt to compensate for something the poor reader cannot do, namely read. Young people try to compensate for their handicap by developing new kinds of behavior, sometimes negative, such as bragging or clowning in front of their classmates. Eventually they may become "behavior problems" in class. This maneuver is executed so that they gain attention while at the same time distracting people from their poor reading. One of the writer's clients had 36 pairs of pants in his closet at home and would wear a different one each day, insisting at the end of

the day that they needed cleaning and pressing. Obviously, the young man displaced his meticulousness from reading to pants. Of course, compensatory mechanisms may have a positive side and provide the individual with much needed relief, but they also distract the poor reader from his goal: reading.

3. *Aggressive Tendencies.* Aggression can show up either overtly or covertly. Overt aggression might be manifested as fighting on the yard as well as becoming a rowdy rascal in a bar. Covert aggression is more refined and shows up more under-handedly, as in crisp, acid remarks made behind the teacher's back. The adolescent with overt aggressive behavior is slanted towards delinquency if things go wrong for him, while the covert aggressive individual becomes more involved in character deviations and social exclusion. His sharp tongue may not be tolerated by his peers unless it serves the group's purpose. Teachers must learn to recognize that these signs of aggression are part of an overall maladjustment problem reflecting a suffering individual who is striking out at what he perceives as a hostile environment.

4. *Anxiety and Withdrawal Tendencies.* Signs of depen-dence, depression, daydreaming, and regression to earlier stages of development are found in this category. A poor reader must be on guard to avoid embarrassing moments. He is constantly vigilant and under tension that results in anxious and appre-hensive reactions. His symptoms are similar to those found in neurotics. Anxiety indicates fear reactions that are out of proportion to the feared object. The very appearance of a teacher with a book under her arm might make him think that it will be his turn next to read aloud in class. The mere admonishment to get ready for Sunday School may evoke anxiety that someone might call on him to read a passage. Behavioral reactions to such anxiety-producing situations may be partial or total withdrawal from the scene. School phobias and high absenteeism can sometimes be traced to withdrawal responses to these anxiety-provoking situations.

Games Poor Readers Play: More Indirect Insight

The idea of playing games—of unconsciously following self-protective patterns of actions and reactions in social situations—was incorporated into a mental health technique by Eric Berne and his associates in California and has become known as Transactional Analysis, or "T.A." for short. The system described in a book called *Games People Play,* was designed for understanding human interactions. T.A. is meant to be used as a preventive-therapeutic technique. It is usually practiced in groups. References can be found in the Appendix.

The advantage of the system is the simplicity of language used in analyzing behavior. While it is not possible here to describe the T.A. system in detail, teachers and parents should be aware of its potential usefulness in understanding the games poor readers play as well as those played by the teachers of these students. Gaining insight and understanding from these games might help them to alleviate some of the emotional strain underlying their symptoms.

1. *Victim Games* include games such as "Kick me!", "Poor Me," or "Wooden Leg." It is obvious that the poor reader sees himself as victimized, a martyr to circumstances rather than to his own failures. Some poor readers simply play the game "Stupid," claiming ignorance whenever they encounter a reading activity. Having been told over and over again that they cannot read well, they might as well claim that they are stupid. If the young adolescent does not receive help which improves both reading level and attitude, he will go on playing "Stupid" forever, on the job and in other life situations. A tragic outlook for a young person, indeed!

2. *Persecutor Games* reinforce the psychological life position of "Not O.K." for the poor reader who is trying to reinforce either his anger or purity. For example, he may fail to read a passage in class correctly and the teacher will say to him "I told you so!" Putting the blame on *him* is the teacher's game. Or, in another instance, a tutor might offer initial praise, then counteract it by criticism. She might begin by saying "Yes, good, but . . .," always rubbing in the idea that she is facing an inadequate partner. In adolescence, poor readers might feel persecuted constantly when people are "after them" to make them read. Angry, acid remarks may be employed to counter the feeling of inferiority.

3. *Rescuer Games* do not intend to make the poor reader confess that he is a failure ("I'm not O.K."). Instead, the teacher tries to justify his or her efforts by saying "I'm only trying to help you!" or "Let me do it for you . . .!" Some teachers who give the poor reader extra help, or parents who assist with homework, assume the role of the Great Rescuer whereby they try to preserve their own integrity, not realizing that in a learning situation *both* parties have to be successful: the teacher *and* the learner.

What can we learn from playing games and understanding their hidden motives? Playing games is actually detrimental to a person because it reinforces existing attitudes and perpetuates them rather than helping the individual to adjust towards normality. Poor readers and adolescents keep on playing games to avoid embarrassment and escape unbearable situations. A young man may successfully excuse himself from reading by going to the bathroom, but he is not being helped with his reading. His games become symbolic of a vicious cycle that must be broken if improvement is to be attained. The tutorial relationship can do much to explain to the suffering adolescent what he is really doing, and what he should be doing in order to make changes. The tutorial relationship is more than mere academic instructions; it is a time and a place where innermost feelings are allowed to emerge in order to be discussed in an honest, anxiety-free, and safe atmosphere. It is an intimate encounter between two sincere human beings. No more, no less.

Relief from these coping maneuvers can be brought about in several ways; the best is remediation of the underlying reading problem. The tutor must be aware of the existence of coping behaviors, both the student's and her own. The student, on the other hand, must understand his problem situations; those in which he "plays games" or employs defense mechanisms. Understanding one's coping behavior is a battle half won. Understanding one's coping behavior, and utilizing effective intervention techniques, is the battle carried to victory.

JUVENILE DELINQUENCY AND READING

The recognition of the interrelationship between learning disabilities and juvenile delinquency has become quite pronounced over the past decades. Many research studies as well as popular magazines report positive correlations. However, one must not jump to conclusions and state that poor reading causes delinquency, or vice versa, since a mere correlation does not allow for causal inferences. Since there is an obvious relationship between reading and adjustment, many institutions for juvenile offenders have set up classes to help their poor readers. They hope to assist these students to correct deficient skills. Hopefully, improvement in reading will mean improved adjustment. This seems to work for the poor reader not as yet in personal trouble, but whether it also works for the poor reader already in trouble remains to be seen.

HOPE FOR POOR READERS

This book cannot be concluded without stressing some of the more favorable and optimistic aspects of poor readers. Where do poor readers end up after they have completed their struggle in school, if they ever complete it? Do they become ditch-diggers, salesmen, executives, fire-fighters, unemployed, or what? Will they be able to hold any kind of job, or will they become "failures" in life wherever they go? Many educators feel, and many parents are afraid, that students with learning disabilities can look forward to only a dim future as far as work is concerned. At least, there will not be a wide choice among occupations and careers open to them due to their reading handicap.

Some poor readers have succeeded by trying doggedly, and they have made it in spite of dim predictions and reduced skills. These students are found to become doctors, bank presidents, engineers, nurses, top-flight salesmen, and others in high-paying positions. They have learned to overcome their poor self-image and make the necessary adjustments. Some have tried once more to learn how to read better after they left school, this time employing mature motivation and adult-oriented teaching methods. It is never too late to begin remediation. In many instances, an adolescent or young adult is more receptive to learning after he has reached a mature stage in life. With a more serious attitude toward learning and a more mature outlook, he is better able to make it the second time around.

One of the comforting thoughts for people with reading problems is that there have been a number of men and women in the annals of history who also were poor readers while in school. They simply had to walk a thorny path during their younger years but made it in the end. Among these famous people who were considered poor readers or learners at one time in their lives are Edison the inventor, Rodin the sculptor, Woodrow Wilson the President, and Einstein the mathematical genius. Then there was Hans Christian Anderson, the beloved story-teller, whose spelling was so bad that his publisher had to get someone to translate his scrambled letters into correct spelling. Among the numerous errors Anderson made were errors in proper nouns, such as Temps (sic) for the river Thames. He used brackfest (sic) for breakfast, and spelled many other words the way they sounded to him. Samples of the way a learning-disabled adolescent writes are shown in the handwriting and spelling of Figures 8-2 and 8-3.

Another famous person and possible candidate for this group and of certain fame was the Prince Imperial, son of Napoleon III. Tutors found it quite difficult to teach the lad how to read and write. After much struggling with tutors, he was finally entered in a school and later received a commission in the British army. However, not all poor readers are the sons of emperors. They may have to buckle down harder in order to get their commissions in life.

What happens to former poor readers? Among the better known studies on what the future holds for language-disabled men is a well-conducted follow-up study by Margaret B. Rawson. Mrs. Rawson published her study in a book titled,

Figure 8-2

Sample Handwriting and Spelling
(Boy, Age 13, IQ 109, Reading on Grade Level)

Supplies	*Supplies*
1. 5-10-5 fertilizer	1. 5-10-5 Feterliser
2. 5 pd. corn	2 5 pd. corm
3. string beans	3. strung beans
4. cucumbers	4. cucumbers
5. watermelons	5 woter mellon
6. radishes	6 radishy
7. cabbage	7 cabag
8. turnips	8 terups
9. tomatoes	9 tondlos
10. cantaloupe	10 cantolope
11. asparagus	11 asspargus
12. peppers	12 peppers
13. potatoes	13 potoes
14. okra	14 acra
15. peat moss	15 Pete mass

Developmental Language Disability, Adult Accomplishments of Dyslexic Boys (Baltimore, Md.: The Johns Hopkins University Press, Inc., © 1968).

Rawson's longitudinal investigation of 56 boys, some dyslexic and some nondyslexic, provides a refreshing and encouraging answer to the question of what happens to poor

Figure 8-3

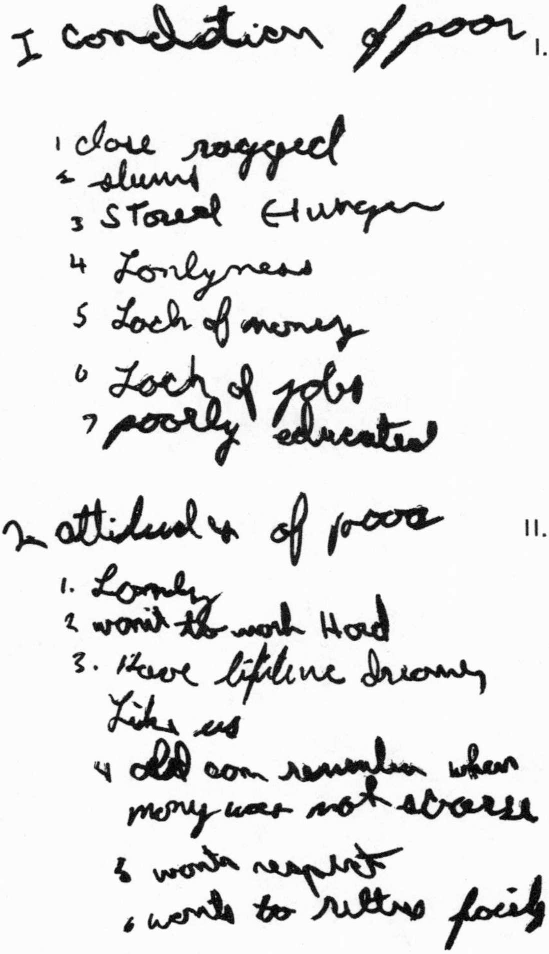

I. Condition of poor

1. clothes ragged

2. slums

3. starved hunger

4. loneliness

5. lack of money

6. lack of jobs

7. poorly educated

II. Attitudes of poor

1. lonely

2. want to work hard

3. have lifetime dreams like us

4. old can remember when money was not scarce

5. wants respect

6. wants to (be) treated fairly

HANDWRITING SAMPLE OF A BOY WITH DYSGRAPHIC CONDITION (POOR HANDWRITING) AND DYSORTHO-GRAPHIC CONDITION (POOR SPELLING); Male, 14 years old, IQ High Average, Good Family Background

readers. It also contradicts the common assumption that poor readers are incapable of performing well in areas requiring language ability. For a period of approximately 30 years, Rawson followed the education and career development of boys from a private school that was one of the first schools to have a comprehensive program for the detection and correction of developmental language disabilities, including poor reading. While the sample of the study might not be very representative of average schools in the United States, certainly not public schools, it nevertheless is very revealing and unique.

Rawson's approach was an objective one under the circumstances she encountered. There were 20 boys who were considered dyslexic; i.e., with low language learning facility. Comparisons were made with the remaining 36 boys and special studies were made with the group called "normal" readers, which included the 20 boys at the upper end of the language learning facility scale. After examining the sociological and psychometric characteristics of her groups, Rawson ranked them on a composite scale of various characteristics demonstrating language disability. Against this background of accumulated data, she presented the study of the adult accomplishments of each of the 56 boys studied.

What were Rawson's findings? She found that dyslexic boys—i.e., poor readers—are not necessarily poor academic and occupational risks. The results of her investigation, in fact, show that dyslexics may be capable of average or even superior achievement in later years. Because verbal skills are so important to educational and vocational success in the modern world, this study should be of interest to everyone working with learning-disabled students. Rawson's findings carry a note of high optimism for people working with adolescents who are still struggling to master the basic skill and art of reading.

Chapter Summary

Older poor readers are in dire need of counseling, guidance, and rehabilitation. Facilities must be made available to them, especially vocational and career guidance, in order to help them find jobs and become productive and fulfilled individuals. Tech-

niques such as behavior modification and counseling can be employed to help both teacher and student cope with problems in relationships that develop in response to learning disabilities.

However, the picture is not quite as dim as it may seem for our older poor readers. Many famous men throughout the world were at one time considered "learning problems." With dogged determination and a new and mature attack on the old problems, they have met with success. A scientifically designed study has shown that students with dyslexic conditions do not necessarily end up as "failures" but can be found in all walks of life and in a variety of positions and occupations. Perhaps your increased efforts to provide help for these students earlier will increase the number of them who go on to enjoy successful lives.

APPENDICES

APPENDIX A

Recommended Readings
Arranged by Chapters

CHAPTER 1   *Looking at a Grave Problem*

Calkins, E.O. (Ed.) *Reading Forum.* A collection of papers concerned with Reading Disability. Bethesda, Md. 20014: U.S. Department of Health, Education, and Welfare. For sale by the Superintendent of Documents, U.S. Government Printing Office, Washington, D.C. 20402. DHEW Publication No. (NIH) 72-44, NINDS Monograph No. 11.

Critchley, M. *The Dyslexic Child,* 2nd ed. Springfield, Ill.: Charles C Thomas, 1970.

Money, J. *The Disabled Reader.* Baltimore; The Johns Hopkins Press, 1966. Chapter 1: "The Epidemiology of Reading Retardation and a Program for Preventive Intervention," by Leon Eisenberg, pp. 3-19.

Report of the Secretary's (HEW) National Advisory Committee on Dyslexia and Related Reading Disorders, *Reading Disorders in the United States,* August, 1969. Reprinted by Developmental Learning Materials, 3505 North Ashland Avenue, Chicago, Ill. 60657, paperback.

Schloss, E. (Ed.) The Educator's Dilemma: The Adolescent with Learning Disabilities. *Academic Therapy Publications,* San Rafael, Calif. 94901. A collection of reprinted articles dealing with reading problems in older students.

Wagner, R.F. *Dyslexia and Your Child.* New York: Harper & Row, 1971. Chapter 2: "What's the Problem?," pp. 14-23.

CHAPTER 2   *Assessing the Reading Problem*

Hoffman, M.S. Early indications of learning problems. *Academic Therapy,* Vol. II, No. 1, Fall, 1971.

LaPray, M. *Teaching Children to Become Independent Readers.* New York: The Center for Applied Research in Education, 1972. Provides a variety of informal assessment devices tested and used at the San Diego State College Clinical Training Center.

Lyman, H.B. *Test Scores and What They Mean.* Englewood Cliffs, N.J.: Prentice-Hall, 1963. A teacher's introduction to the different kinds of tests and their underlying theories and assumptions. Glossary of Terms included in Appendix.

Martin, H.P. Vision and its Role in Reading Disability and Dyslexia. *The Journal of School Health,* Nov., 1971.

McGlannan, F.K. Familial Characteristics of Genetic Dyslexia: Preliminary Report from a Pilot Study. *Journal of Learning Disabilities,* Vol. 1, No. 3, March 1968.

Miller, W.H. *Diagnosis and Correction of Reading Difficulties in Secondary School Students.* New York: The Center for Applied Research in Education, 1971. Presents guidelines for assessing older poor readers and setting up a remedial program at the secondary level.

_____. *Identifying and Correcting Reading Difficulties in Children.* New York: The Center for Applied Research in Education, 1971. Contains simple reading tests and projective techniques especially designed for poor readers.

_____. *Reading Diagnosis Kit.* New York: The Center for Applied Research in Education, 1974. Provides a complete survey of all standardized and informal tests used in reading diagnosis today. Includes many ready-to-use diagnostic devices.

Minskoff, E.H., Wiseman, D.E., and Minskoff, J.G. *Inventory for Language Abilities.* Ridgefield, N.J.: Educational Performance Associates, 1972. An assessment inventory based on learning deficiencies modeled after the Illinois Test of Psycholinguistic Abilities (ITPA).

Schain, R.J. *Neurology of Childhood Learning Disorders.* Baltimore: The Williams & Wilkins Co., 1972. A survey of neurological dysfunctions and diseases possibly involved in some learning disabilities. Relatively nontechnical introduction to the subject.

CHAPTER 3 *Establishing a Tutorial Relationship*

Quandt, I. *Self-Concept and Reading.* Newark, Del.: International Reading Association, 1972.

Rauch, S. (Ed.) *Handbook for the Volunteer Tutor.* Newark, Del.: International Reading Association, 1969.

Smith, C. (Ed.) *Parents and Reading.* Newark, Del.: International Reading Association, 1971.

Wagner, R.F. Secondary Emotional Reactions in Children with Learning Disabilities. *Mental Hygiene,* Vol. 54, No. 4, October 1970, pp. 577-579.

CHAPTER 4 *Choosing Basic Approaches to Remediation*

Chall, J. *Learning to Read: The Great Debate.* New York: McGraw-Hill, 1967. A thorough introduction to the various approaches to teaching reading, and a documented discussion of phonics versus word recognition methods.

Frostig, M. and Maslow, Ph. *Learning Problems in the Classroom.* New York: Grune & Stratton, 1973. The authors take a total look at the student when considering his learning disabilities.

Trela, T.M. *Fourteen Remedial Reading Methods.* Palo Alto, Calif.: Fearon Publishers, 1968. Contents of soft-cover book are relevant to Chapters 4 and 5. It gives a survey of existing methodological approaches to teaching reading without referring to specific publishers.

Wagner, R.F. *Teaching Phonics with Success.* Johnstown, Pa.: Mafex Associates, 1960. An introduction to auditory and phonetic training, followed by exercises and games.

CHAPTER 5 *Selecting Specific Remedial Techniques*

Barsch, R. *Perceptual-Motor Curriculum.* Seattle: Special Child Publications of the Seattle Seguin School, Inc., 1967.

Buchanan, C.D. and Sullivan Associates, *Programmed Reading.* New York: McGraw-Hill Book Company, 1963. A series of programmed readers.

Cheyney, A. *Teaching Reading Skills Through the Newspaper.* Newark, Del.: International Reading Association, 1971.

Critchley, M. *Developmental Dyslexia.* Springfield, Ill.: Charles C Thomas, 1964.

Dawson, M.A. *Teaching Word Recognition Skills.* Newark, Del.: International Reading Association, 1971.

Gattegno, C. *Words-in-Color.* Chicago, Ill.: Encyclopedia Britannica, 1962. A color-coded method of phoneticizing the English alphabet.

Gillingham, A. and Stillman, B. *Remedial Training for Children with Specific Disabilities in Reading, Spelling, and Penmanship.* Cambridge, Mass.: Educators Publishing Company, 1956, 1960.

Heckelman, R.G. Solutions to Reading Problems. San Rafael, Calif.: Academic Therapy Publications, 1974.

Heineman, R.B. *The Fourth R: A Return to Learning for Side-Tracked Adolescents.* Boston, Mass.: Beacon Press, 1967.

Herr, S. *Learning Activities for Reading.* Second Edition. Dubuque, Iowa: Wm. C. Brown Company, 1970. Soft cover, a well-structured manual for teachers and tutors. Many examples for exercises and games.

Horn, T. (Ed.) *Reading for the Disadvantaged: Problems of Linguistically Different Learners.* Newark, Del.: International Reading Association and Harcourt, Brace, 1970.

Langford, K., Slade, K., and Barnett, A. An Examination of Impress Techniques in Remedial Reading. *Academic Therapy,* Vol. IX, No. 5, 1974, pp. 309-319.

Levin, J. *Classroom Activities for Encouraging Reluctant Readers.* New York: The Center for Applied Research in Education, 1974. A soft-cover handbook providing tested individual and group activities for stimulating interest in reading.

Mallet, J.J. *Classroom Reading Games Activities Kit.* New York: The Center for Applied Research in Education, 1975. Provides over 100 simple, easy-to-make games for developing more than 30 specific reading skills.

_____. *Reading Skills Activity Cards.* New York: The Center for Applied Research in Education, 1975. 240 separately printed, individualized activities for reinforcing skills in eight major areas.

Miller. W.H. (Ed.) *The Reading Clinic.* New York: The Center for Applied Research in Education, Inc., 1974. Innovative, classroom-tested techniques and materials for reading instruction, for use with individuals and groups. Monthly publication.

Money, J. (Ed.) *The Disabled Reader.* Baltimore, Md.: Johns

Hopkins Press, 1969. A detailed introduction to many specific reading techniques; e.g., Words-in-Color, VAKT, and i/t/a.

Montessori, M. *The Montessori Method.* New York: Schocken Books, 1964.

Orton, S.T. *Reading, Writing, and Speech Problems in Children.* New York: W.W. Norton, 1937.

Read, R.C. *Tangrams—330 Puzzles.* New York: Dover Publications, Inc., 1965. Paperback.

Thompson, R. *Energizers for Reading Instruction.* West Nyack, N.Y.: Parker Publishing Co., 1973. Many practical hints and devices to motivate the poor reader.

CHAPTER 6   *Comprehending What Is Being Read*

Barber, J.W. *The Book of 1000 Proverbs.* New York: The American Heritage Press, 1971.

Dawson, M.A. *Developing Comprehension—Including Critical Reading.* Newark, Del.: International Reading Association, 1968.

Furth, H. and Wachs, H. *Thinking Goes to School.* New York: The Oxford Press, 1974. Practical methods for teaching thinking based on Piaget's theories.

Herber, H. *Developing Study Skills in Secondary Schools.* Newark, Del.: International Reading Association, 1965.

Levi, A. Remedial Techniques in Disorders of Concept Formation. *The Journal of Special Education,* Vol. 1, No. 1, 1966, pp. 3-8.

Pulaski, M. *Understanding Piaget.* New York, N.Y.: Harper & Row, 1971.

Schwebel, M. and Raph, J. *Piaget in the Classroom.* New York, N.Y.: Basic Books, 1973.

The Mott Basic Language Skills Program, Comprehension Series. Galien, Mich.: Allied Education Council, 1968. A series of programmed readers.

Wagner, R.F. *Successful Devices in Teaching Study Habits.* Portland, Maine: J. Weston Walch, 1961. Soft cover, study workbook for students also available from same publisher.

Zimbal, S.F. *Reading Comprehension—Lessons and Tests.* New York, N.Y.: Amsco School Publications, 1972. A very useful soft-cover booklet giving a variety of reading paragraphs with comprehension questions at the end of each paragraph.

CHAPTER 7   *Organizing and Planning Remedial Reading Programs*

Cooper, T.L. Filing's the Name, and Order's the Game. *Teaching Exceptional Children,* Summer 1973, pp. 180-189.

Figurel, A. (Ed.) *Better Reading in Urban Schools.* Newark, Del.: International Reading Association, 1970.

Katz, A.H. *Parents of the Handicapped; Self-Organized Parents' and Relatives' Groups for Treatment of Ill and Handicapped Children.* Springfield, Ill.: Charles C Thomas, 1961.

Patterson, G.R. and Gullion, M.E. *Living with Children.* New Methods for Parents and Teachers. Champaign, Ill.: Research Press Company, 1971.

The Wisconsin Design for Reading Skill Development, 4401 West 76 Street, Minneapolis, Minn. Company provides the basic design and test materials to establish a complete remedial reading program into which existing materials and techniques can be absorbed.

Woburg, L. *Inservice Teacher-Training in Reading.* Newark, Del.: International Reading Association, 1972.

CHAPTER 8   *Coping with Poor Readers: The Affective Domain*

Andersen, K. *Classroom Activities for Modifying Misbehavior in Children.* New York: The Center for Applied Research in Education, 1974.

Ansara, A. Language Therapy to Salvage the College Potential of Dyslexic Adolescents. *Bulletin of the Orton Society,* Vol. 12, 1972. Also available as Reprint No. 48 from the Orton Society, Inc., 8415 Bellona Lane, Towson, Md., 21204.

Campos, L. and McCormick, P. *Introduce Yourself to Transactional Analysis.* Berkeley, Calif.: Transactional Publications, 1972.

Ernst, K. *Games Students Play.* Millbrae, Calif.: Celestial Arts Publications, 1972.

Feriden, Jr., W.E. *Classroom Management Through the Application of Behavior Modification Techniques.* Linden, N.J.: Remediation Associates, Inc., 1970.

Glavin, *Behavioral Strategies for Classroom Management.* Columbus, Ohio: Chas. E. Merrill Publ. Co., 1974.

Harris, T.A. *I'm OK—You're OK:* A practical guide to transactional analysis. New York: Harper & Row, 1969.

McMillan, D.L. *Behavior Modification in Education.* New York: The Macmillan Co., 1973.

Pitts, C.E. (Ed.) *Operant Conditioning in the Classroom.* New York: Thomas Y. Crowell, 1971.

Rawson, M.B. *Developmental Language Disability.* Adult Accomplishments of Dyslexic Boys. Baltimore: The Johns Hopkins Press, 1968.

Reynolds, G.S. *A Primer of Operant Conditioning.* Glenview, Ill.: Scott, Foresman and Co., 1968.

Skinner, B.F. *Science and Human Behavior.* New York: MacMillan, 1953.

Stephens, T.M. *Behavioral Approaches in the Schools.* Columbus, Ohio: Chas. E. Merrill, 1974.

Thompson, L.J. Language Disability in Men of Eminence. Available as Reprint No. 27 from the Orton Society, Inc., 8415 Bellona Lane, Towson, Md. 21204.

Valett, R.E. *Modifying Children's Behavior.* A Guide to Parents and Professionals. Palo Alto, Calif.: Fearon Publishers, 1969.

Wagner, R.F. Games Dyslexics Play. *Academic Therapy,* Vol. IX, No. 1, Fall, 1973.

Wagner, R.F. *Modern Child Management. A Behavior Modification Program for Parents and Teachers.* Johnstown, Pa.: Mafex Associates, 1975.

Wagner, R.F. and Guyer, B.P. Maintenance of Discipline through Increasing Children's Span of Attending by Means of a Token Economy. *Psychology in the Schools,* Vol. VIII, No. 3, 285-289, July 1971.

Williams, D.L. and Jaffa, E.B. *Ice Cream, Poker Chips, and Very Goods.* Distributed by: The Maryland Book Exchange, 4500 College Avenue, College Park, Md. 20740. Paperback.

Woburg, L. *Inservice Teacher-Training in Reading.* Newark, Del.: International Reading Association, 1972.

APPENDIX B

Recommended Professional Journals

Name and Publisher	Content	Issue
Academic Therapy 1539 Fourth Street San Rafael, Calif. 94901	Interdisciplinary journal directed to an international audience of teachers, special teachers, parents, and specialists working in the field of reading, learning, and communication disabilities. All ages. Methods of identification, diagnosis, and remediation emphasized.	Issued six times per year, September, October, December, February, March, and June.

Bulletin of the Orton Society
8415 Bellona Lane
Towson, Md. 21204

Official bulletin by the Orton Society, a nonprofit scientific and educational organization for the study and treatment of children with specific language disability (dyslexia). All ages, international in scope. Many useful reprints available.

One issue annually.

The Journal of Learning Disabilities
5 N. Wabash Avenue
Chicago, Ill. 60602

Multi-disciplinary, primarily concerned with learning disabilities (diagnosis and treatment). All ages, international in scope. Theoretical and practical contributions.

Issued monthly. June/July and August/September combined.

Journal of Reading
International Reading Association
6 Tyre Avenue
Newark, Del. 19711

Primarily directed to classroom teachers, the journal also concerns itself with older poor readers and motivational techniques. Its purpose is to exchange information and opinions regarding reading skills.

Eight times annually, October through May.

The Journal of Special Education
Buttonwood Farms, Inc.
3515 Woodhaven Road
Philadelphia, Pa. 19154

Primarily devoted to all types of handicapped children in a special setting, the journal contains relevant material for remedial reading approaches.

Quarterly.

Reading Clinic
The Center for Applied Research in Education, Inc.
521 Fifth Avenue
New York, N.Y. 10017

Directed to Grade 1-8 classroom teachers and reading specialists, this practical publication provides tested activities and materials for both developmental and remedial reading programs. Includes ready-to-use activity worksheets for diagnosing specific weaknesses and reinforcing specific skills.

Ten monthly issues, September through June.

Reading Newsreport
Multimedia Education, Inc.
11 West 42nd Street
New York, N.Y. 10036

Covers broad spectrum of reading problems and includes articles of interest to the remedial reading teacher; e.g., tutoring relationship, use of comic books in class, etc.

Monthly issues, October through May.

The Reading Teacher
International Reading Association
6 Tyre Avenue
Newark, Del. 19711

Primarily directed to elementary school teachers, the journal also brings articles on remedial reading. Occasionally it deals with problems such as minimal brain dysfunctions, paraprofessionals, and motivational techniques.

Eight times annually, October through May.

Slow Learner Workshop
Parker Publishing Company, Inc.
West Nyack, N.Y. 10994

Primarily directed to elementary educators, this publication provides practical, tested techniques and activities for teaching children with all types of learning difficulties. Includes successful new ideas and programs from across the country.

Ten monthly issues, September through June.

APPENDIX C

Publishers of High-Interest, Low-Vocabulary Resource Materials

Name and Address of Publisher

Notes and Comments (Titles, Price, Etc.)
(For Use by Teachers to Record Up-to-Date Information as Received from Publishers Upon Inquiry)

Academic Book Service, Inc.
The Academic Building
West Haven, Connecticut 06516

Addison-Wesley Publishing Co.
2725 Sand Hill Road
Menlo Park, California 94025

Allied Education Council
Distribution Center
P.O. Box 78
Galien, Michigan 49113

Allyn & Bacon, Inc.
470 Atlantic Avenue
Boston, Massachusetts

American Book Company
300 Pike Street
Cincinnati, Ohio 45202

Amsco School Publications
315 Hudson Street
New York, N.Y. 10013

Bantam Books, Inc.
School Division
666 Fifth Avenue
New York, N.Y. 10019

Benefic Press
10300 W. Roosevelt Rd.
Westchester, Illinois 60153

Bowmar
622 Rodier Drive
Glendale, California 91201

Center for Applied Research
in Education, Inc.
521 Fifth Avenue
New York, N.Y. 10017

Continental Press, Inc.
2085 E. Foothill Blvd.
Pasadena, California 91109

Curriculum Associates
247 Washington Street
Wellesley, Massachusetts 02181

T.S. Denison
5100 West 82nd Street
Minneapolis, Minnesota 55437

Developmental Learning Materials
7440 Natchez Avenue
Niles, Illinois 60648

The Economy Company
P.O. Box 687
Stone Mountain, Georgia 30083

Electronics Futures
27 Dodge Avenue
North Haven, Connecticut 06473

Fearon Publishers
Lear Siegler, Inc.
Education Division
6 Davis Drive
Belmont, California 94002

Field Educational Publishers
2400 Hanover Street
Palo Alto, California 94304

Garrard Publishing Company
Champaign, Illinois 61820

Grolier Educational Corporation
845 Third Avenue
New York, N.Y. 10022

Holt, Rinehart and Winston, Inc.
Box 3323
Grand Central Station
New York, N.Y. 10017

Houghton Mifflin
1900 Batavia Avenue
Geneva, Illinois 60134

Imperial International Learning
Box 548, Rt. 54 South
Kankakee, Illinois 60901

Interpretive Education
400 Bryant Street
Kalamazoo, Michigan 49001

Intext Press
257 Park Avenue South
New York, N.Y. 10010

Lawson Book Company
9488 Sava Street
Elk Grove, California 95824

The Macmillan Company
539 Turtle Creek South Drive
Indianapolis, Indiana 46227

The Macmillan Company
School Division
Riverside, New Jersey 08075

Mafex Associates, Inc.
Publishers
111 Barron Avenue
Johnstown, Pennsylvania 15906

McGraw-Hill Book Company
Webster Division
Manchester Road
Manchester, Missouri 63011

New Readers Press
P.O. Box 131, University Station
Syracuse, N.Y. 13210

Noble and Noble, Publishers, Inc.
750 Third Avenue
New York, N.Y. 10017

Prentice-Hall Learning Systems, Inc.
Dept. Cl, P.O. Box 47X
Englewood Cliffs, N. J. 07632

Pyramid Publications
Educational Division
9 Garden Street
Moonachie, New Jersey 07074

Reader's Digest Services, Inc.
Educational Division
Pleasantville, N.Y. 10570

Scholastic Book Services
904 Sylvan Avenue
Englewood Cliffs, New Jersey 07632

SRA
259 E. Erie Street
Chicago, Illinois 60611

Stock-Vaughn Company
P.O. Box 2028
Austin, Texas

Troll Associates
320 Route 17
Mawah, New Jersey 07430

William Morrow and Co., Inc.
Lothrop, Lee and Sheppard Co.
School & Library Service Dept.
105 Madison Avenue
New York, N.Y. 10016

World Traveler
P.O. Box 479
LaSalle, Illinois 61301

Xerox Corporation
600 Madison Avenue
New York, N.Y. 10022

Index